ANTOSHA AND MASHA

The Chekhovs in Yalta

ANTOSHA AND MASHA

The Chekhovs in Yalta

A play in four acts
by Mark Perry

Based on the lives of

Anton Pavlovich Chekhov
(1860-1904)

and

Maria Pavlovna Chekhova
(1863-1957)

DRAMA CIRCLE
Chapel Hill, North Carolina

Drama Circle
P.O. Box 3844
Chapel Hill, NC 27515 USA

Email: info@dramacircle.org
Website: www.dramacircle.org

The play *Antosha and Masha* is available for your group to produce. Visit the Drama Circle website for information on royalties and to apply for permission. No performance may be given without written permission.

Cover Image: "Garden in Yalta: Cypress Trees" (1886)
by Isaak Levitan (1860-1900)

Book 1 of the 19 X 19 CHALLENGE

Antosha and Masha: The Chekhovs in Yalta

ISBN: 978-1-953219-01-5
Library of Congress Control Number: 2026908109

26 27 28 29 30 31 10 9 8 7 6 5 4 3 2 1

Introduction

Many of us theatre folk have a special affection for the Russian playwright Anton Chekhov. Although he only left four mature, full-length plays, each is a masterpiece and each has a contingent of us arguing why it is the best one. My pick would be *The Cherry Orchard*, and each semester I take time to persuade a class of undergraduates of its value—with mixed results.

The genius of Chekhov's work is not readily apparent to the reader. His plays at first feel random, speech-filled, depressing mostly but with an odd absurd outburst, and there's all these people lounging about with impenetrable Russian names. And yet that very combination, when given a certain stage treatment, produces a spellbinding effect.

Antosha and Masha is a play about the Chekhov household written in homage to Chekhov's inimitable style. This is both in the play's form, which mixes the serious and comic, and in its content, as the characters discuss aesthetics and the "opening into eternity" his work invokes. It also documents, in some measure, the genesis of *The Cherry Orchard,* even as it mirrors the early sunsetting of the writer's life in Yalta.

What binds the story together, however, are the family relationships, and the most important relationship of his life was arguably the one with his sister, Mariya Pavlovna. Masha was dedicated to her brother, and Anton trusted her as he trusted no one else. His was the artistic genius, but hers was the steady hand that managed a large, chaotic household and a literary legacy operation lasting many decades after his death. Through revolution and world wars, she carried forward the torch of his art.

This play is intended as a historical dramatization and not the freer form of historical fiction. The details of the lives, the nature of the characters, the timelines are about as close as I could bring them to historical fact and still have a coherent play. Dramatic license has been used with dialogue, of course, as well as conflation of time and event.

Where there is less historical accounting available on individuals, such as the servants, I invited Chekhov's archetypes to fill the space. This includes the characters of Marfa, Uncle Nikolai, Mustafa, Ivan and to an extent Chekhov's mother, Evgenia. I tried to give each a spark of life within the story's landscape of love and loss, heartbreak and transcendence.

Unlike a Chekhov play, *Antosha and Masha* is intentionally didactic. I am a fan of plays where you learn things and are not merely swept about by emotion—where you immerse in a different age, soaking in the personalities and historical details, while contemplating the relevant big questions.

One might certainly cut the play by 15 minutes or more by excluding discussions of art and mysticism. That would deflate my pedagogical intent, but I understand time and attention are dear. Otherwise, I hope the ideas prove enjoyable to the theatre lover and at least tolerable to any theatre goer.

Thanks to those who read the script and offered notes and encouragement, and appreciation to those who participated in readings: our drama circle, the company from *The Seagull*, Julia Gibson and the PATP actors, and Jeri Lynn Schulke and Redbird Theatre. Acknowledgment must be made of the historians and scholars who have provided such detail and insight into Chekhov's life and work. Special gratitude goes to Chekhov scholar Radislav Lapushin for his attention to the script and for his gently offered suggestions. Eternal thanks as always to my wife, Azadeh, and to my parents.

MP

March 2026

ACT BREAKDOWN

ACT I: December 1899. Very early morning, before dawn. Chekhov's study in the "White Dacha", a home still under construction.

ACT II: April 1900. A sunny afternoon. Chekhov's study and the yard outside.

ACT III: April 1902. A spring morning. A parlor, a porch and a garden.

ACT IV: April 1904. Sunset. The parlor.

PRODUCTION NOTE

Throughout the play, Anton has advanced tuberculosis (aka, TB, consumption), a lung-centered disease that has a persistent cough. How much coughing is not strictly dictated in the script, but a lifelike amount might be overwhelming on stage for both actor and audience. Instead, it is recommended you choose your coughing bouts, and the actor may emphasize the character's struggle to restrain coughing. This also applies to the character Levitan, who appears in Act 2.

SETTING: Yalta, Crimea. The Chekhovs' house at Autl

TIME: 1899 – 1904.

DRAMATIS PERSONAE

(Cast Minimum: 4F;4M. Maximum: 5F;7M)

MASHA
Maria Pavlovna Chekhova

EVGENIA
Evgenia Morozova Chekhova
Mother to Masha and Anton

OLGA
Olga Leonardovna Knipper-Chekhova. An actress

MARFA
A maid

MARIUSHKA
An old nanny

ANTON
Anton Pavlovich Chekh

NEMIROVICH
Vladimir Nemirovich-I
A director

LEVITAN
Isaak Ilyich Levitan
A painter

GORKY
Alexei Maximovich F
Maxim Gorky. A wr

UNCLE NIKOL
Marfa's uncle

MUSTAFA, a Tat

IVAN, a grocer's

INTENDED DOUBLE-CASTINC

OLGA & MARIUSHKA

MUSTAFA & NE

UNCLE NIKOLA

IVAN & LEVITA

ACT I

December 1899. Yalta—a resort town in Crimea. It is very early morning, before dawn.

A study in the "White Dacha", a home still under construction. Embers glowing in a fireplace are the only source of light or warmth in the room. You can barely make out the exquisite wooden interior that is mostly empty of furniture.

A cushy lounge chair is pulled up close to the fire, and a man sleeps on it. He's covered in two down blankets and his feet are up on an ottoman. His breathing is raspy, and his sleep is uneasy, as he constantly suppresses a persistent, tubercular cough. This is ANTON CHEKHOV, *a few weeks before his 40th birthday.*

He mumbles in a dream.

ANTON: (*Barely audible.*) My life is gone as if I'd never lived it. My life is gone...

He is then silent again.

The sound of keys at a door. A woman, in her mid-30s, walks in. She wears traveling clothes and moves like someone who has caught a second wind after a day and night of travel. This is MASHA, *Anton's sister.*

MASHA: Antosha?

ANTON *coughs, but doesn't wake up.* MASHA *walks towards him.*

MASHA: You must be freezing.

She goes to the fire, puts a log on it and prods it with the poker. The light grows some. She lights a candle, and we see the room better. There is a large table with papers and books stacked high on it and a small table near Anton with its own stack. More papers and books are stacked along the sides of the walls, in some sense of order.

There are stacks of telegrams and letters, as if they're early in the process of being filed.

MASHA *turns to look at her brother, whose condition startles her.*

MASHA: Oh dear brother. (*Puts her fingers to her eyes to stop tears from coming.*) Bags.

She walks back towards the door, speaking to ANTON *as if he were awake, but not so loud as to wake him up.*

MASHA: What kind of help do you have here? I got out of the cab, I rang the bell, woke up your gardener, or maybe he was praying ... (*opens door, retrieves bags from just outside the door.*) So he comes out, hands me the key and heads right back in. No offer to carry my bags, or my trunk, which is still down at the end of the drive. (*Directly to* ANTON.) I've gotten used to the treatment I'm getting in Moscow.

She picks up from the table Anton's infamous pince-nez glasses, sees how dirty they are, and wipes them with her handkerchief.

MASHA: Treatment I'd never receive if I wasn't the sister of the most famous writer in Russia. (*Kisses his head.*) Okay, most famous after Tolstoy.

ANTON *sits up, looks at her.*

ANTON: Mama? What are you doing up?

MASHA: Have I grown so old I look like our mother to you?

ANTON: (*Waking, but weak.*) Masha, you've arrived.

MASHA: Yes. (*Gently places the pince-nez on his nose.*)

ANTON: (*Goes to get up.*) Sorry we couldn't be there to pick you up.

MASHA: Rest, Antosha, I'm right here.

ANTON: There's your face. You look healthy. (*Suppresses a cough.*)

MASHA: Well, I've been busy. Moscow is a beehive, and I feel a bit like a queen, or a duchess at least: I'm having salons, I go to the theatre, I paint, and I'm surrounded by artists and society people. I feel like every poisoned memory of Melikhovo is being slowly extricated from my brain: the chaos, the mud, the mouths to feed, the peasants quarreling, bridges collapsing, escaped convicts on the loose!

ANTON: My memories of Melikhovo are mostly good.

MASHA: You were hardly there this year.

ANTON: No I was here. In exile.

MASHA: Making our new home.

ANTON: (*Through coughs.*) And yet it seems Crimea gets cold too, and the stoves the architect put in barely work.

He stands up, but looks wobbly.

MASHA: I'll contact him. Let's get this fire going. (*Goes to get wood.*)

ANTON: How long can you stay?

MASHA: (*Off.*) How much have you been coughing?

ANTON: (*Hedging, pokes at the fire.*) It's just a cold.

MASHA: (*Entering with wood.*) And you're paper thin, haven't you been eating? (*Begins working on fire.*)

ANTON: I have, and I would have gained a few pounds if it weren't for the spigot installed in my posterior that undoes on the back-end all the good that I do on the front-end. (*Smiles and suppresses his cough by sheer will.*) And that might not be so bad if not for the hemorrhoids the size of grapes. But I'm alive. Much to the surprise of the reading public. (*Shivers and pulls one of the down blankets around him.*)

MASHA: Living here in Yalta was supposed to help.

ANTON: Living here has made me keenly aware of the necessity of companionship.

MASHA: Mama writes you have lots of visitors.

ANTON: That's company not companionship.

MASHA: (*Standing up, tending to him.*) Sure. But Yalta and Moscow: this could be it, the balance we've been looking for. I have a fine apartment and the house here is coming along. The train comes as far as Sevastopol, although you could have chosen a more accessible spot...

ANTON: Accessible means more visitors. How long are you here?

MASHA: A week.

ANTON: A week?

MASHA: You don't like visitors.

ANTON: Look, neighbors and friends, intellectuals and idiots, relatives and every woman I ever flirted with, they all crush in, and how can I rest? How can I work? But Masha, you and I, we've kept this family, this whole enterprise going. I earn the money, but you've been the rock.

MASHA: Being the rock is hard. It's nice just being myself.

ANTON: I'm on the board of the local school here, we can arrange a teaching job here for you.

MASHA: I'm taking painting lessons again, and learning so much.

ANTON: How is Olga?

MASHA: I'd like to paint a little this week. You know, my trunk is down the end of the drive.

ANTON: It'll be fine.

MASHA: It's nearly in the street. That servant of yours was no help.

ANTON: No one will bother it, this is not Moscow.

MASHA: Anton, who runs the show here?

ANTON: Clearly not me. How is Olga?

MASHA: (*Looking through the telegrams and letters.*) Olga is ... charming, brilliant. She's dazzling them all as Yelena now, just as she did with Arkadina.

ANTON: I wish I could be there.

MASHA: You say that, but there's a thousand things in the production that will vex you.

ANTON: Tell me Stanislavski isn't playing Astrov like a limp noodle. But did Olga send anything? Will she come?

MASHA: She told me emphatically to tell you emphatically, yes.

ANTON: But when?

MASHA: Nemirovich casts her in every show. In the Hauptmann play, and in 'Julius Caesar'.

ANTON: They all come to see Olga.

MASHA: (*With some distance.*) She's not as beautiful as some, but onstage she is magic.

ANTON: Yes.

MASHA: And ... audiences can't get enough.

ANTON: I can't get enough. I can't get any, in fact. But then, look at me ... (*Ironically.*) I used to be a sought-after bachelor in Moscow society.

MASHA: (*Picking up his irony.*) Oh, the MOST sought-after bachelor—

ANTON: Flattery at this stage is like spreading peach jam on a wrinkly old sausage.

MASHA: What?

ANTON: I don't know, I don't know how to joke any more. The servants don't understand it. Everyone who comes to visit is either wretched, in need of a handout, or so full of sympathy, I fall into playing the role of elderly statesman, as if every word might be the author's last.

MASHA: It's not so grim as that. Right?

ANTON: I still have a will to live. I think. If nothing else, I have to get this all off to the publisher, Marx.

MASHA: Your life's work is worth over twice what he paid you!

ANTON: Marx will make sure the work is right.

MASHA: But then you send that nincompoop Sergeenko as your agent.

ANTON: Masha, let's not quarrel. I've missed you. Do you know how many people in this town, in this country, I can trust?

MASHA: You really don't understand how many people love you.

ANTON: I didn't say love. You must be exhausted. (*Getting up, shakily.*) Let me get the fire going in your room.

MASHA: I'll, I'll do it. I slept some on the train. Please, Antosha.

He relents. She sits and looks at him, again overwhelmed. She looks at the papers and books spread out.

ANTON: There's an army out there, digging up everything I've ever written.

MASHA: Every last skeleton.

ANTON: Yes, skeletons! With their ghosts still! And when you leave, they'll fill the air again. I had no grasp how many words I have plagued the world with, I figure 400, 500 stories—all to feed the tummies of you wretched ones.

She smiles. He picks up a story on old yellowed paper.

ANTON: Now to fill them again, I unearth each and every corpse. To adjust a word or a phrase or to rewrite six pages, I have to relive each story, each haunted reflection of my past. (*Pause.*) Or, if the fire is getting low ...

He gestures throwing the story on the fire.

MASHA: Please don't even joke about that. I'm guessing the cupboards are empty. You have a working telephone now, don't you? (*Going off.*) We have one in our building. Let me call the grocer.

ANTON: (*Wryly.*) I wholeheartedly believe that if I burned this story here, tomorrow morning, it would march its way in attached to some young grave robber in muddy shoes, who doesn't take time to wipe his feet because he is certain he has just rescued a priceless treasure from the maw of oblivion.

MASHA: (*Off.*) And he would be right.

ANTON: What is this greed for stories? They're everywhere, like petulant children at the door, crying to be let in, but open that door: as they fly in, peace of mind flies out. And the conception of children is the only fun part. The rest is labor, toil and disappointment—Oh, Mama asked you to wake her when you arrived, but wait, her sleep isn't the best. (*Looks at the story in his hands, then:*) Did Olga send nothing?

MASHA: (*Off.*) She did. It's in the trunk, down at the end of the drive.

ANTON: Well, wake the servants, I must have it right away.

MASHA: (*Reentering.*) You act like you're joking.

ANTON: As Papa said, they don't make servants like they used to.

ANTON & MASHA: "Not remotely like when we Chekhovs were serfs!"

MASHA: Some of us still work like we are—Now I'm feeling the trip.

Sounds from inside the house.

ANTON: Someone is stirring. That might be Marfa.

MASHA: The new maid? (*Exits towards the kitchen.*)

ANTON: New is right. Sweet, but it's like training a newborn.

MARFA *enters, sleepy.*

MARFA: Good morning.

MASHA: Good morning.

MARFA: Oh, pleased to see you, mistress. (*Does a little curtsy.*)

MASHA: Thank you, how are we doing with food?

MARFA: (*Yawning.*) We have a few potatoes.

There's a knock internally.

MARFA: I'll get it. (*Exits.*)

MASHA: Goodness. So I phoned the grocer and spoke to a very sleepy young man, who said he'd be right over.

ANTON: Impressive.

MARFA: (*Reentering.*) Dr. Chekhov, Mr. Mustafa is here. He's looking for your gun.

ANTON: I'd hardly call it <u>my</u> gun, but it's in the shed. The bullets are in here.

MARFA *exits;* MASHA *reenters.*

ANTON: Masha, do you remember this?

He hands her the story he was holding earlier.

MASHA: "'The Ideal Gentleman' by Antosha Chekhonte."

ANTON: It's from when I was 23 and a medical student. Mama found it in a trunk.

MASHA: (*Reading the attribution.*) "To my sister, Masha, because she is nineteen and sad and believes that her life is over now that the long-legged boy she has been flirting with for three months has gone and married a buck-toothed lady of the gentry..." This was never published, was it?

ANTON: You don't remember! I described in detail the ideal man worthy to marry you—sitting on a 17-hand horse, with the sunset perpetually behind him, and how he would never fall for another woman, bucktooth or not, even if she did have an annuity of 10,000 rubles.

MASHA: I remember a story where you described the perfect man, but it was you, quality by quality, measurement by measurement.

ANTON: That was the joke! That I was the ideal gentleman.

MASHA: Yeah, it's very foggy.

ANTON: Because you read it once, started bawling and told me never to write you another story. But Mama saved it.

MASHA: (*Starts to go.*) Sweet. I'll read it, maybe tomorrow...

ANTON: I'll print it up on gold-embossed paper and give it to you on your wedding day.

MASHA: (*Turns to him, smiles.*) Thanks. (*Beat.*) Your Schmul sends his undying affection.

ANTON: Levitan! How is he?

MASHA: (*A deep breath.*) His doctor said he's got a year, maybe less. But who knows.

ANTON: Who knows.

MASHA: He asked again.

ANTON: What did you say?

MASHA: I didn't.

ANTON: So you would?

MASHA: Marry for love?

ANTON: Marry a dead man so you can help plan his funeral.

MASHA: Not dead.

ANTON: What makes you think he would be faithful? He's been with a thousand women.

MASHA: You're one to talk. (*A beat.*) I'm sorry. I believe he has only proposed to me.

ANTON: Yes, but is it because of you or because of me?

MASHA: What? Anton, he loves me.

ANTON: Love, love, I'm talking about trust. Frankly, I don't know what all of you see in us writers and painters and musicians.

MASHA: Would you give your blessing?

ANTON: Levitan wants a wife out of Balzac, not a nice girl like you.

MASHA: He wants some comfort at the end of a long journey. You know?

ANTON: It's up to you, Masha.

MASHA: So you don't approve.

ANTON: I didn't say that.

MASHA: Seven years ago, Alexander Smagin, that kind man, asked for my hand, and you demurred just like this.

ANTON: Look, I just woke up.

MASHA: (*After a beat.*) Olga Knipper will marry you. With the right approach.

ANTON: Marry a dead man so she can help plan my funeral. I have you for that. (*Starts coughing.*)

MASHA: (*Looking out a window.*) It's stuffy in here. It's balmy outside, you can smell the sea. Look at all the trees you've planted.

ANTON: Cherry trees! And almond, and mulberry, some bamboo. I've become a gardener. It's good to find your true calling before you return to the earth.

MASHA: I love the moonlight in the trees. Look, it looks like our mother walking through the trees, arms lifted, dancing in the moonlight.

ANTON: We have two cranes making a home out there. Imagine.

MASHA: (*Looks again.*) Wait, that is Mama! What is she doing out there?? In a nightgown!

ANTON: She gets hot sometimes.

MASHA *tries to open the doors to the garden, but they won't open.*

MASHA: What's wrong with this door?

ANTON: We need to get that fixed.

MASHA: It is not safe for her out there! She'll freeze!

ANTON: She comes in when she's ready.

MASHA: Or she'll get robbed!

ANTON: There's no one out there except Mustafa.

MASHA: This is your mother!

ANTON: (*With a bit of heat.*) My dear, she is much healthier than her doctor, and I'm trying to keep him alive.

MASHA: What? You're her doc— (*Realizing, moved.*) Why do you do that?

ANTON *jiggles the handle a bit and the door opens.* MASHA *is out the door.*

MASHA: Mamochka! What are you doing out here?

EVGENIA: Masha, you've come! Why did you take so long?

MASHA: Mama, I have students—children who depend on me.

EVGENIA: Just give them a good grade, and come tend to your family.

MASHA: Would you please come inside?

EVGENIA: You're hungry. There's soup that Mariushka made, but it's not good. I'm worried about Antosha. Look how skinny he is.

MARFA *has entered, extending to* ANTON *a ceramic mug.*

MARFA: Coffee, sir?

MASHA: Mama, your nightgown is inside out!

EVGENIA: Oh it doesn't matter.

MASHA: What chaos is this? We're not villagers.

ANTON *having sipped the coffee, spits it out. Everyone reacts.* MASHA *grabs the cup.*

MARFA: Oh oh ohhh, I screwed it up!!!

ANTON: Did you forget to grind the beans?

MARFA: I'm sorry, please don't fire me.

ANTON: It's fine.

MASHA *seethes.*

EVGENIA: Masha, did you bring it? The icon?

MASHA: Yes, Mama, but it's in my trunk which is out at the gate, because I can't find anyone to help me bring it in!

MARFA: Oh Uncle Nikolai can get that.

MASHA: Does he work here?

MARFA: No, but he's always willing to help. He's waiting outside.

MASHA: Ask him to come in.

MARFA: He prefers being outdoors. When he was young, he once had to spend a cold night in a crypt. He's also a little embarrassed; he hasn't been in a home of the gentry before.

MASHA: We're not gentry, and if he's your uncle, he must get used to coming in. What's his patronym?

MARFA: Alexeyevich.

MASHA: (*Off, calling out.*) Nikolai Alexeyevich, please come inside and warm up!

UNCLE NIKOLAI *enters. He is tall and stoops despite the high ceilings. He bows multiple times.*

UNCLE NIKOLAI: Greetings, greetings, hello, dear friends, hello. Sorry to interrupt.

MARFA: Uncle, would you get the mistress's trunk? It's at the gate.

UNCLE NIKOLAI: Yes already done. (*He pulls it from just outside the door.*) I walked by and I thought that is no place for a trunk, no, someone left it here hoping for a helping hand.

MASHA: Thank you so much. (*Extends a tip.*)

UNCLE NIKOLAI: (*Repelled.*) Oh I could never. We're just so grateful Marfa has been conscripted to such an esteemed individual.

(*Bowing, trying to make eye contact with* ANTON.) The good doctor, I'd give him my liver.

MARFA: Uncle that's enough.

ANTON: (*Drily.*) I need lungs not a liver.

UNCLE NIKOLAI: I can give you one of those too, if you need, or two.

MARFA: Uncle.

ANTON *smiles at him.* MASHA *goes to open the trunk.*

MASHA: I also brought the candlest—

MUSTAFA, *the gardener, enters with a gun. He has an uncertain smile, as if he could be friend or foe. Everyone stops.*

MUSTAFA: The bullets?

ANTON: (*Indicating.*) In that cabinet.

He goes to get the bullets. He smiles at EVGENIA, *as he puts bullets in the gun.*

EVGENIA: Infidel.

MUSTAFA: Your mother thinks I'm an infidel, Anton Pavlovich. Please assure her that I say my prayers five times a day. And in between, I do the work of the Lord.

MARFA: Oh I don't like it when he shoots the cats.

ANTON: If the dog would do his job.

MUSTAFA: It doesn't help that someone is feeding the cats.

EVGENIA *scowls at him and exits.* MUSTAFA *cleans the gun with a rag.*

UNCLE NIKOLAI: Everything in good balance. You know, sir, as they say, When the cat's away, the mice will play.

MARFA: Uncle, that's not a saying about balance.

UNCLE NIKOLAI: Will you listen? Your pupil thinks she's the teacher now.

MARFA: I'm not his pupil.

MUSTAFA *exits.*

UNCLE NIKOLAI: I've read about Dr. Chekhov in the paper, how he's a builder of schools all over and libraries. This man values education.

ANTON: My sister is the teacher.

UNCLE NIKOLAI: The modestness! I read how you came from such beginnings as many of us, and school was the key to your upraisement. I myself attended to fourth grade when I had to go work the fields, and I learned my letters and numbers, and this is how we rise in the world. That's what her auntie and I want for Marfa. She didn't take to school so well, so this—being in the person of such a valued presence—this is just golden.

MASHA: Nikolai Alexeyevich, why don't you have a seat? Okay—

UNCLE NIKOLAI: Thank you very much.

He doesn't sit. EVGENIA *reenters with* MARIUSHKA, *the old nanny. Having opened the trunk,* MASHA *takes out a fur hat and puts it on* ANTON*'s head.*

MASHA: From Olga.

ANTON: That's grand! And so warm.

MARIUSHKA *kisses* MASHA.

EVGENIA: Masha, the icon!

MASHA *pulls out an object covered with a cloth. She reveals the icon of St. John the Divine.* EVGENIA *takes it with devotion and places it on a shelf. She is moved.*

MASHA: Lovely. Now maybe we can all get a couple hours of shuteye.

EVGENIA: Children, let us pray, let us pray for your father.

EVGENIA *kneels.* MASHA *goes along.* ANTON *sits and gets a steely look.* MARFA, NIKOLAI, *and* MARIUSHKA *kneel.*

EVGENIA: In the name of the Father, the Son, and the Holy Spirit. In the name of the holy saints, and St. John the Divine, who I see before me. I would like to speak to my husband.

ANTON: (*To* MASHA.) She speaks as if it were a telephone.

EVGENIA: Pavel, you— you were not a good husband, and you were not a good father, but I won't deny your moments of virtue. I worry for your soul, because you died so soon. A certain length of suffering is essential in this world to prepare us for the next life. This is what the lives of the Saints show us. You only had a day or two, Pavel, and you had a heavy load of sins to burn away.

MASHA: (*Quietly.*) Mama, go easy.

ANTON: She's been bottling this one up a while.

UNCLE NIKOLAI: (*To* MARFA.) She's quite earnest, isn't she? And why not, no need for beating around the bush with the next life.

MARFA: (*Hushing him.*) Uncle.

EVGENIA: Pavel, I worry for the souls of our children. Kolia, who struggled so and now is with you. Aleksander, who drinks. Vania is sweet, but his family. Misha, he's Misha. Little Evgenia, I don't worry for her. God protects His angels and keeps them close, but the rest He lets wander and toil until we make our way back to Him.

UNCLE NIKOLAI: Very wisely said, mistress.

MARFA: Shhh...

EVGENIA: I will bear some suffering for your sake, Pavel, but not too much. You should burn a little bit, or a little bit more than a little bit, to atone for the hard times you put your family through. Okay, I'm finished with you, Pavel. I'll speak to God now.

UNCLE NIKOLAI: A woman who knows what she wants.

MARFA: Uncle...

EVGENIA: Dear God, please forgive my children, and my grandchildren: I'd like to say their names, if I can remember. I'm not fond of them all but it is my duty to pray for them in case no one else will: little Mosia, who passed away, and Kolia and Anton and ... Volodia, and what's Aleksander's other one?

MASHA: Mikhail.

EVGENIA: Right, that one. Forgive them, they are not at fault for their parents' poor character and bad decision making.

UNCLE NIKOLAI: Never heard the like of this, a whole new method of praying!

EVGENIA: (*Clears her throat.*) And God, please bless Masha and Antosha, they have loved and respected their parents, they have held the family together. Help them both to find spouses to marry and not just ... nincompoops and floozies.

MASHA *and* ANTON *almost laugh.* MUSTAFA *has entered quietly.*

EVGENIA: Help them so they may raise happy children. We need happy children in this world, God. And these are my best two—the pick of the litter. And I think they are ready to settle down and make a family. Right? (*She turns around to check with them.*)

MASHA: Yes, mother, if it's His will.

ANTON *looks at his mother with care.* EVGENIA *smiles at him.*

EVGENIA: (*With tears.*) God. Heal my dear Anton. You know the disease. And you know the cure. And Mashenka, things will be better now she's here. Amen. I'm going back to bed.

She stands and exits. Silence.

MUSTAFA: Anton Pavlovich.

Everyone jumps.

MUSTAFA: The cat got away.

He empties the bullets into the cabinet. MARIUSHKA, MARFA *and* UNCLE NIKOLAI *rise.* ANTON *and* MASHA *remain, they hold hands. A bell in the distance.*

UNCLE NIKOLAI: The most extraordinary woman. What a light! She shineth and the world filleth with radiance.

MARFA: Uncle, I heard the bell at the gate. Would you mind?

UNCLE NIKOLAI: (*As he moves to the door.*) Dr. Chekhov, I see where you get your heart! I read this about you—but they say that Anton Pavlovich Chekhov, he cares, he cares for the little people, no displays, no speeches, but he's got heart, and NOW I can tell them where he gets it.

MARFA: Uncle, the gate.

UNCLE NIKOLAI: Yes yes. (*Starts to go, turns back.*) If I had as much faith as that woman, I wouldn't have such a bad time letting go of your auntie, because I would know I can talk to her just like that, just save up to buy an icon, look St. John in the eye, and I can talk just like I would if she was right in front of me. I wouldn't have to feel like I'm not saying the right words, or I'm being judged for, well, you understand.

There's a knock off. MUSTAFA *inspects the icon, skeptically.*

UNCLE NIKOLAI: Such a busy place at 4:30 in the morning.

He exits. MASHA *goes with him.*

MARFA: (*To* ANTON.) I'm sorry.

ANTON: Has your auntie passed?

MARFA: Oh no! But she has been quite sick. With the consumption.

ANTON: Ah. Does she see a doctor?

MARFA: She did once, but it didn't help.

MASHA *enters with* IVAN, *who carries a sack full of groceries.* MUSTAFA *exits.*

MASHA: This is the sleepy boy I woke up with the phone call.

IVAN: Yes Ma'am. I'm Ivan.

MASHA: Well, Ivan, we appreciate you coming so quickly.

IVAN: My father would do anything for Dr. Chekhov. He says he's a great man, and he pays his bills.

MASHA: Wait, just one second and I'll get your money. Anton?

ANTON: Ah, right.

They go off.

MARFA: Sleepy boy, you're good looking. You could be an actor.

IVAN: I was in a school play and I didn't like it.

MARFA: So do you like being a grocer?

IVAN: No I hate it. And I hate my father. He makes me watch the store all day.

MARFA: What about your mother?

IVAN: She's dead.

MARFA: Me too. Mother and father.

IVAN: Sorry.

MARFA: But I have love in my life.

IVAN: That's nice.

MASHA *and* ANTON *reenter, with cash.*

MASHA: Marfa, please show Ivan to the pantry.

MARFA: Happy to.

The two exit. ANTON *coughs.*

ANTON: Only a week? When does school start back?

MASHA: It's not just that, Anton. I have a life, appointments...

ANTON *continues coughing.*

MASHA: (*Delicately.*) If we could arrange a slightly larger allowance for me, I wouldn't need to teach. I could visit more, be more flexible.

ANTON: (*Through coughs.*) A career is more than money...

MASHA: Please lay down, Antosha. I'll go oversee this business. Then I'll get a bit of rest.

ANTON: I'll help you get the fire going.

He suppresses the cough. MASHA *sees blood on his handkerchief.*

MASHA: Oh there's blood. Please, no. Please just ... I'm here. I'll take care of you. We'll put some flesh back on this skeleton. Get you back to your Ideal Gentleman measurements. And then we'll send you off to marry Olga.

MASHA *goes to leave.*

ANTON: Masha. Do you trust her?

MASHA: They're a Bohemian lot, and everyone seems to know about her affair with Nemirovich, even his wife suspects. But ... Olga is smitten by you.

ANTON: Smitten!

MASHA: Can she trust you? You get bored pretty quickly.

ANTON: I'm a monk. The piano and I, neither of us are played upon these many months.

MASHA: Mama would prefer you marry a plump young religious girl.

ANTON: (*Looking at the window.*) I have this image stuck in my head. The flowering branch of a cherry tree poking through a window in an old manor house. Life and death, civilization and revolution, it's all there.

MASHA: (*As if she's been holding back on this information.*) They said they'd come—the Art Theatre—to Yalta. On their tour in Spring.

ANTON: That's wonderful! Olga told you?

MASHA: Well, Nemirovich, but she was there. Now I'm going to blow out this candle. Please rest.

ANTON: Oh I want to write her a postcard before the sun comes up.

He takes a pen and postcard from the table beside the chair.

MASHA: Nighty night, Antosha.

She blows out the candle and exits.

ANTON: It's too dark. (*Takes the pages of the story from earlier.*) 'The Ideal Gentleman.' Easy come...

He smiles and places the story on the fire to make enough light to write his postcard.

ANTON: (*As he writes.*) Olga dear, Masha's just arrived and said the gift you sent was stolen—by a rogue flock of geese traveling north for the winter. Send yourself, or at least one of your vital organs, right away.

He smiles softly, suppresses a cough. Lights fade.

End of Act I

In between acts, the actor playing OLGA *comes out and plays from a Chopin nocturne on the piano.*

Before Act II begins, someone calls out "Olga!" And she rushes off.

ACT II

Chekhov's study and the yard outside. The doors are open. It is sunny afternoon in late April 1900.

The study is now fully furnished, more organized, but open books and unfinished projects abound.

In the yard, a MAN *is asleep on a bench, which is actually a set piece from 'Uncle Vanya', left here as a memento. The man's features are covered by a dark coat. If we hear him at all, it's through his heavy breathing.*

The maid, MARFA, *is seated at some distance from him, staring.* UNCLE NIKOLAI *is busying himself with yardwork. An offstage phone rings twice.*

MARFA: Dr. Chekhov is not going to like this. It's one thing if a vagrant dies in a ditch, it's another if he dies in the yard of a famous person. They'll make it into a scandal, worse than the time he insulted Yalta in a telegram and the operator shared it with the newspaper. Everyone was upset at Dr. Chekhov because he called the city, well, I didn't quite get it, but I assumed he was calling it a dump. If you're going to share your true feelings, you don't want to do it with everyone listening, and I don't think Yalta's a dump, I think he was just lonely. (*Turning to sleeping man.*) Oh, I hear him breathing. That's good—Why don't you say something, Uncle Nikolai?

UNCLE NIKOLAI *pays no attention.*

MARFA: So I think Dr. Chekhov is just used to the busy-ness of city life. When you're famous, I think you always need people paying attention to you and noticing you and sending you messages and gifts and when you don't get that, you start to get cranky. And you might take it out on the place where you live or the people there, but really I think if you're unhappy, you can complain about wherever you are. I don't know why he's so lonely, he has his mother. What more does he want? (*Begins to cry.*)

UNCLE NIKOLAI: (*Sharply.*) Stop your sniveling.

MARFA: I don't know why I'm so emotional.

UNCLE NIKOLAI: Oh you don't know why you're so emotional? And don't be talking about Dr. Chekhov and his life, you need to be thinking on your own life and the shame you've brought on our family. And thinking doesn't mean talking.

MARFA: I have to talk to think; I can't sit quietly and get anywhere, the thoughts just stay stuck in my head.

UNCLE NIKOLAI: Well, all your talk is about Dr. Chekhov, not yourself and your condition. This is why famous people are miserable, because everyone avoids their own problems by talking about the problems of a writer or an actor, when all they want to do is share their art with us. They didn't invite us to sit and watch their lives like it's some sort of entertainment. And I'm not talking to you! And when you refer to Dr. Chekhov, you must say "your excellency" as he has been bestowed upon himself a special rank by the Tsar.

MARFA: By the Tsar??

UNCLE NIKOLAI: Or some of the higher ups anyway.

MARFA: I called him "your excellency", and he said it was silly.

UNCLE NIKOLAI: You stupid girl, I should bash you on the head.

She starts to cry again.

UNCLE NIKOLAI: I didn't say I was going to, I said I should. (*Moved.*) We tried to raise you right, your auntie and me. We struggled to train you, and you throw your legs wide open for an oaf that drives a mule.

MARFA: He's not an oaf!

UNCLE NIKOLAI: He's not a count! Who's going to marry you now? With no dowry, you're just a clog of hair circling the drain.

MARFA: I'm sorry, uncle.

UNCLE NIKOLAI: I'm taking you home.

MARFA: No Uncle, I like it here. It's not unnormal for a serving girl to have a baby in a household like this.

UNCLE NIKOLAI: You're not here to be helped by them, you are the help! You can't do that with a brat running up and down the halls of a famous writer. Who is sick! Who you could learn from, and raise yourself up in the world. I should bash your head.

He goes out. MARFA *cries.*

ANTON *enters hurriedly from the house, carrying a mouse by the tail, followed by* MASHA *and* NEMIROVICH, *who is laughing.*

MASHA: You need to take it to the cemetery. It will come back!

ANTON: I know!

ANTON *walks out into the yard and out of sight. He looks healthier than in Act I.*

MASHA: We need a cat!

ANTON: (*Off.*) No cat!!

MASHA: (*Referring to man.*) This one's still here—Who's been touching my art supplies?

MARFA: Not me, mistress.

MASHA: One of the cranes maybe? (*Packing up the paints.*) Please tell the cranes to put the caps back on the tubes when they're done—Marfa, we need you in the kitchen.

MARFA: Sorry, Mistress, I need to meet with Dr. Chekhov about a delicate matter.

The phone rings off.

MASHA: We have a house full of guests and Mariushka's gout is acting up. (*Exits.*)

MARFA *curtseys to* NEMIROVICH. *He is a classy individual—incisive, yet good-humored. He smiles. They wait for* ANTON *in the study.* MARFA *can't help but gawk.* ANTON *reenters.*

ANTON: Nemirovich, forgive me the interruption!

NEMIROVICH: Oh I quite enjoy seeing the distinguished author in his pastoral setting.

ANTON: Let me just finish what I was saying about the performance—(*Seeing* MARFA.) Have you seen my spectacles?

MARFA: (*Curtsies, speaks formally.*) No. Dr. Chekhov, I would like to meet with you briefly to discuss a matter of some delicacy.

ANTON: (*With an ironic smile.*) Okay—give me ten minutes.

MARFA: (*Still with formality.*) That would be fine. I will come back in 10 minutes.

She goes.

ANTON: Okay, can we talk about Stanisla—

MASHA: (*Reentering.*) They're calling with every single telegram. Don't mind me. (*Goes to her painting.*)

NEMIROVICH: What are you painting?

MASHA: Ha. It's an iris I started last week, it had an extraordinary color, and I almost got it, but it has since wilted. (*Packing up.*)

NEMIROVICH: Could you recreate it from memory?

ANTON: Yes, like the once beautiful woman, now middle-aged, who labors with makeup, lighting, and charm to revive what has all but slipped away.

MASHA: You're such a chauvinist sometimes.

ANTON: I speak of my soul, my dear.

MASHA: Clever. But as Mama says: clever won't help you on Judgment Day.

She starts to go. NEMIROVICH *stops her.*

NEMIROVICH: Maria Pavlovna, I don't know what was passing between you two, but you are no wilted flower. (*Kisses her hand.*)

MASHA: Oh.

She exits, blushing a bit. ANTON *and* NEMIROVICH *exchange a look, then:*

ANTON: NOW—Stanislavski is a creature of preternatural enthusiasm and creativity. He's a dear soul, he spends hours assuring me in person and in correspondence that he intends to do the greatest service to my plays. He dedicates hours to training the crickets and frogs to come in on cue, and yet I don't remember ever writing a line or a stage direction intended for a cricket.

NEMIROVICH: Audiences love the crickets.

ANTON: Keep the crickets, the problem is this nastroenie mood thing everyone is seizing on—this lugubrious pacing, these gloomy people who stand there motionlessly, as if he is casting the play in amber. My characters are people, not wax figures. People move around, they fidget, they pick their nose. (*Pointing.*)

NEMIROVICH: I wasn't.

ANTON: Why doesn't he understand my plays the way I intend them? I am not writing in Chinese, I don't use difficult words. As a playwright, I am at heart a vaudevillian. This is what I loved to watch in the theatre as a young person. So I write on the title "Comedy". The plays are filled with irony and silliness, I have Uncle Vanya—a role he plays himself—say "Bang Bang" while he's shooting a gun.

NEMIROVICH: And you end the play with him in a despairing limbo with no possibility of escape—"we shall rest." Stab me in the heart!

ANTON: (*Dismissively.*) Aaah!

NEMIROVICH: You have Kostya shoot himself in 'The Seagull', and Ivanov does the same. These are not your farces like 'The Bear' or 'The Wedding'.

ANTON: But take a hint from those farces what my intention is! The plays are closer to that than—forgive me—the funeral processions Stanislavski offers up for the sentimental rabble.

NEMIROVICH: You can hardly call ...

ANTON: Look, you asked me my honest opinion! I am deeply honored by the company coming here—for the expense, for the time, and all for the sake of this consumptive hermit and the people of Yalta, who have never seen such exquisite performances.

NEMIROVICH: So we bring the mountain to Muhammad, and Muhammad says, this is not the mountain I want.

ANTON: (*Ironically.*) Watch it, my gardener is Muslim.

NEMIROVICH: You artists are never content, and you have no reliable perspective on your work!

ANTON: Are you not an artist?

NEMIROVICH: Anton, I watch with my jaw dropped how Konstantin Sergeyevich shapes your plays into these striking metaphors, these meditations on life and death, and it's like Shakespeare...

ANTON: Spare me the eulogy.

NEMIROVICH: Except it's closer because it's Russian, and it's modern, and yes they're funny, I get that, he doesn't, but that doesn't mean that the work he's doing isn't some of the greatest theatre we've ever seen.

ANTON: Are you friend or flatterer?

NEMIROVICH: And you sit there in the audience squirming like a schoolboy and moving your eyes up in the air.

ANTON: I thought I was quite constrained.

NEMIROVICH: When Olga is up there, but give Vishnevsky his moments too.

ANTON: When Olga is up there, all eyes are on her.

A beat.

NEMIROVICH: Well, yes. I knew that from the moment she first auditioned for the Philharmonia.

ANTON: So what choice did you have but to give her every leading lady role from Sophocles to Hauptmann?

NEMIROVICH: (*A bit uncomfortable.*) That's true.

ANTON: You're wearing her out.

NEMIROVICH: She can always say no.

A beat. OLGA *bursts through the doors. She is 31 and has an unusual energy and striking charisma.*

OLGA: Oh you're both here.

She looks back and forth between them, then smiles and bleats like a goat before backing out of the room and closing the doors. ANTON *and* NEMIROVICH *laugh. The phone rings.*

NEMIROVICH: She's quite taken with you.

ANTON: And yet I feel like a guest arrived late to a party ... already in full swing.

NEMIROVICH: Have a dance. Plenty of punch to go around. (*Changing the subject.*) What did you think of the reciting of Maxim Gorky's poem? It was quite a hit today.

ANTON: The proletarian uprising is a popular theme.

NEMIROVICH: Voice of the common man.

ANTON: I like him. He's been coming to visit. He seemed personally offended at the price Adolf Marx gave me for my complete works. Said he was going to demand more money for me, or else he'd buy Marx out.

NEMIROVICH: We'd like to produce his plays.

ANTON: Oh?

MASHA: (*Off.*) Vladimir Nemirovich!

NEMIROVICH: (*Getting up.*) No need for jealousy, we'll always make room for you. BUT I NEED 'Three Sisters' soon!

MASHA *enters briskly.*

MASHA: Our retinue is out the door and making final bows. Anton, they're asking for you. (*Hands him his pince-nez.*) And someone found this by your seat in the theatre.

ANTON: Masha, are you really going with them?

MASHA: We talked about this! I need to get back.

The phone rings, she exits. NEMIROVICH *start to go.*

ANTON: Wait wait, I have something for you.

At the bookshelf, he pulls out a gold medallion shaped like a book.

NEMIROVICH: Oh what is this? "You made my Seagull fly." That is so dear. I feel like Trigorin.

ANTON: I'm your Nina, "if you should ever want me, come take me." (*Laughs, coughs, touches* NEMIROVICH'*s lapels.*) They warned me about these moiré silk lapels of yours.

They shake hands.

ANTON: (*Moved.*) After that debacle in Petersburg, I uh ... I was ready to give up writing plays.

NEMIROVICH: You don't get away that easy.

NEMIROVICH *goes out.* ANTON *coughs more.* MASHA *reenters.*

MASHA: (*Concerned.*) Do you want me to make an excuse for you?

ANTON: No no, I'll come. Is Olga gone?

MASHA: She's in the kitchen with Mama, complimenting her outfit and trying to explain the creaking stairs last night.

ANTON: I should slip Mama some Valerian before a rendezvous.

MASHA: Don't tell Olga that, she'll believe you'd do it. Did you ask her? (*No response.*) What are you waiting for?

ANTON: We talk about it, around it. The words somehow don't penetrate into the arena of ... actuality.

MASHA: I can give you three minutes with her, but we have a train to catch. And you have about three days of rest to catch.

ANTON: I feel good. Floating on air.

MASHA: Right. (*After a beat.*) Even if I stayed, it could only be a few days. What you need is more help. Paid help!

ANTON: You're right.

MASHA: If you want me more often, my salary isn't much to cover.

ANTON: Why don't you take the teaching job here?

MASHA: I don't live here!

MASHA *exits.* ANTON *steadies himself, holding the table.* OLGA *peeks in.*

OLGA: (*Bleating like a goat, and quite accurately.*) Baah, baah.

ANTON: Have you been studying the goats next door?

OLGA: (*Sweeps in.*) How could you tell?

She hugs him and kisses him on the cheek, hangs on him. He seems strengthened in the moment.

ANTON: Are you really going? Why don't you make an honest man of me and stay forever as my concubine? We'll keep visitors away by leaking scandalous stories to the papers, and I'll send my mother on a tour of the Caucasus. What do you say?

OLGA: I love to play the Delilah.

ANTON: How long are you indentured to Nemirovich?

OLGA: (*Quick fury.*) I'm indentured to NO ONE.

ANTON: I ... I just meant the Theatre.

OLGA: (*Cooling down.*) I'm free most of June. Sorry. I control what I do. No man, not Nemirovich, not my father—may he rest in peace, and not you. As long as you know that. (*Smiles.*)

ANTON: (*Voice starting to quaver.*) I don't want to let you go. (*Turns away.*) Sorry, it's just the whirlwind of these ten days.

OLGA: I like that you're open to me. It's just, I have commitments.

ANTON: And I have a date with destiny, as they say.

OLGA: (*Grabs him by the vest, like a character in a play would.*) Then I will fight off that destiny! Like a banshee.

ANTON: You will, will you?

OLGA: (*Bearing her teeth.*) Ay ay, captain.

ANTON: Captain?

She growls, like a wildcat.

ANTON *stands to his full height, lifts her up in the air, and she puts her legs around his hips, and they go to kiss, but he coughs.*

ANTON: (*Through coughing.*) So sorry.

MASHA *is there at the door.*

MASHA: Mama's coming.

ANTON *suppresses the cough.* EVGENIA *enters, comes right in and stands between* OLGA *and* ANTON, *with her back to Olga deliberately and with no subtlety. Phone rings,* MASHA *exits.*

EVGENIA: Antosha. Nadia Ternovskaia is at the front door, asking about your health.

ANTON: That's kind. You can tell her I'm fine, just a little tired from all the fuss.

EVGENIA: She wants to see you.

He sighs.

EVGENIA: Maybe I can invite her for tea with me, and you can just pass by, when you get a moment, make a little conversation.

ANTON: (*Feigning interest.*) Okay, and what should I say?

EVGENIA: I don't know, ask her about her mother, you always want to get in well with the mother.

OLGA: That's true.

MASHA *reenters.*

ANTON: Yes. And is there anything particular I should say, any phrase you think will be effective?

EVGENIA: You're the writer, you can come up with something.

ANTON: Oh I'm the writer! I thought you were casting me in this play of yours.

EVGENIA: What are you talking about? You're spending so much time around these theatre people with all their flash and charm, and you forget about a perfectly good girl like Nadia. She is a good Christian—her father's an archpriest! And I don't need to tell you how beautiful she is, and how young, and how head over heels she is about you. I don't know what else you're looking for. (*Looks at* OLGA.)

OLGA: It's true, Anton, what else are you looking for?

EVGENIA: A house needs children.

ANTON: You have grandchildren, Mama, and they will visit.

EVGENIA: They're far away. And frankly, some of my children aren't so sure how to be parents, they're still children themselves. And when children raise children, the little ones spoil. Like a jar of jam that isn't properly sealed. But you two, I'm putting my hope in you as parents!

She grabs onto MASHA *and* ANTON. *Out of respect,* OLGA *heads outside.*

EVGENIA: Imagine. Bringing children into this world that will know love and stability and kindness and gentleness. They will rise above this clinging, complaining that these young people do these days. They will be children of God. (*Through tears.*) It is not too late. I thought we were losing you, Antosha, but your health is better. Plant your feet somewhere, this running around you do is too much. You come back and you're rail thin, coughing and spitting up blood. What is this disturbance inside of you that makes you run? Plant your feet, just like you're planting these trees out here. This is how you grow, this is how you heal. Look at all these beautiful women who come to your door every day.

MASHA: We call them Antonovkas.

EVGENIA: If you don't like one, choose the other, but choose one. Do you think I was thrilled to marry your father? That old horse face?

They laugh.

EVGENIA: You laugh, but I had no dowry! And I wasn't laughing. Forgive me, and may God forgive him, but without your father, I would not have you—my children and my dearest treasures, even the half-baked ones, and we wouldn't be here having this moment, our hearts swelling, and our tears flowing down. Antosha, any one of these lovely ladies will give you lovely children, you just have to settle somehow. Settle. That part of your soul that escaped when your father was beating you. It's time for him to come home.

MASHA: Okay, Mama, I think that's enough.

EVGENIA: And Masha, we just have to find some sort of man for you.

MASHA: You mean there aren't a host of men begging to marry me?

EVGENIA: What about the man who was just here? He was very charming, he kissed my hand.

MASHA: Vladimir Nemirovich is married, Mama.

They look at OLGA, *now at the door. She redirects to the sleeping* MAN.

OLGA: Who's this?

ANTON: We don't know.

EVGENIA: Is he dead?

OLGA: He's breathing.

ANTON: (*Under his breath.*) Maybe he wants to marry Masha.

MASHA *slaps his arm.*

EVGENIA: I'm going to invite Nadia in for tea. What you do is up to you, Antosha.

ANTON: Fine.

Stirred up, ANTON *wanders off into the garden, alone.* EVGENIA *starts to go, but* MASHA *stops her.*

MASHA: Mama, please don't think I'm powerless. I have somebody in mind, and I'm ... taking steps.

EVGENIA: That's good, Mashenka. Tell Anton, and he'll talk to the boy.

She exits. MASHA *turns, sees* OLGA *and smiles. A beat.*

OLGA: Should I be concerned?

MASHA: About Nadia? (*Slight chuckle.*) Your bags are ready, yes?

OLGA: I'm an actress, my dear, but I'm also German. When do you have to be back at school?

MASHA: Mrs. Rzhevskaia is expecting me Tuesday at 8 AM.

OLGA: GAH!

MASHA: I'm jealous of those of you who do art as a profession.

OLGA: Teaching is noble, and living life can be an art.

MASHA: Yeah yeah.

OLGA: Okay. You want to know the secret to making a life as an artist? Are you ready for it? (*Draws* MASHA *in.*) You're willing to sacrifice everything. Family. Friendship. Love. Everything.

MASHA: Certainly it's not as desperate as that.

The phone rings.

OLGA: But, Masha, you're not even willing to give up that phone call, are you?

The phone rings again. MASHA *squirms inside.*

OLGA: This is your exam. Can you sacrifice something as stupid as copying down a dull telegram he's not going to read anyway?

The phone rings. They are locked in a stare. ANTON *enters.*

ANTON: Masha, can you get that?

MASHA: UGGHHHH!!!

She goes and OLGA *laughs.* ANTON *comes in and sits.*

ANTON: You're a dangerous one: You had me going and my mother came in, we have a house full of guests...

OLGA: Including Nadia Ternovskaia.

ANTON: No doubt Mama is now arranging the wedding decorations.

OLGA: (*Coyly.*) So you're saying I have to fight for you?

MASHA *is at the door, putting on her coat. She calls* ANTON *over.*

MASHA: Look, when I go, you have to rest. I'll take the phone off the hook. It will take time to get the house back into shape, but let them do it. (*Quietly.*) If we arrive on time, I'll go straight to see Levitan. His last letter broke my heart.

ANTON: (*Snapping a bit.*) The man has THREE women looking after him—a mother and her two daughters!

MASHA: Are you jealous of a dying man?

ANTON: (*Quietly.*) I don't know what I'm doing. I'm in a spin. I'm like one of the helpless dupes in my stories I used to smirk at.

MASHA: You've been in love a hundred times. How's this different?

The phone rings. MASHA *and* ANTON *stare at each other for several rings. Then* MASHA *breaks, exits.*

MASHA: Fine.

Meanwhile, OLGA *has quietly begun to make adjustments to herself and the room, as if preparing the mood to a performance. She is masterful in this element.*

ANTON: What are you doing?

OLGA: Fighting.

She closes the door, takes her position. She turns, instantly exuding the jealous passion of Arkadina from 'The Seagull.'

ANTON: Are you going to perform?

OLGA: "Am I so old and ugly already that you can talk to me like this with no shame about another woman?" (*Embraces* ANTON, *who is both enchanted and embarrassed.*) "Oh, you have lost your senses! My splendid, my glorious friend! You are the last chapter of my life." (*Falls on her knees.*) "You are my pride, my joy, my light." (*Embraces his knees.*)

ANTON: Someone might come in.

OLGA: (*Breaks character.*) That line comes later. (*Instantly back to Arkadina.*) "I could never endure it should you desert me, if only for an hour; I should go mad. Oh, my wonder, my marvel, my king!" (*Breaks character.*) Now.

ANTON: (*Somewhat playing along.*) "Someone might come in."

OLGA: (*Gets up, as Arkadina.*) "Let them come! I am not ashamed of my love."

MASHA *has opened the door and come in, slipping off her coat. She understands what's happening.* OLGA *takes her hand.*

OLGA: (*Kissing* MASHA*'s hand.*) "My jewel! My despair!" (*Back to* ANTON.) "You want to do a foolish thing, but I don't want you to do it. I won't let you do it! You are mine, you are mine! This forehead is mine, these eyes are mine, this silky hair is mine. All your being is mine."

ANTON: Okay it's getting hot...

OLGA: (*Her finger to his lips.*) Chup.

MASHA: Suffer what you put your characters through.

OLGA: (*Continuing.*) "You are so clever, so wise, the first of all living writers; you are the only hope of your country. You are so fresh, so simple, so deeply humorous. You can bring out every feature of a man or of a landscape in a single line, and your characters live and breathe."

MASHA: Is this for Trigorin or yourself?

OLGA: (*Especially sincere.*) "Do you think these words are just flattery? Do you think I am not speaking the truth? Come, look into my eyes; look deep; do you find lies there? No, you see that I alone know how to treasure you. I alone tell you the truth."

MASHA: Wonderful.

EVGENIA *is at the door, sees* OLGA, *holding* ANTON*'s face, looking deep into his eyes.*

EVGENIA: What's going on?

MASHA: (*Whispering.*) Shhh... Olga is performing from 'The Seagull.'

EVGENIA: What? Anton! Nadia waited outside for forty-five minutes and now she's waiting inside. This is not one of your doctor's appointments!

She exits. OLGA *is still committed to the moment.* ANTON *squirms.*

ANTON: I think I should...

OLGA: "My dearest, you will go with me? You will? You will not forsake me?"

ANTON: (*Extricating himself.*) What's Trigorin's line? "I have no will of my own ..." I don't remember. (*Goes to leave.*)

MASHA: (*Reciting.*) "Is it possible that women like that?!"

ANTON: (*To* OLGA.) I need to use the wash room.

He exits, shaking and steadying himself on MASHA *as he passes.*

OLGA: (*Still as Arkadina.*) "Now he is mine."

This last line doesn't land quite right with MASHA.

OLGA *lets the character go, smiles at* MASHA, *who applauds.*

MASHA: Wow, what a nutjob she is, right?

OLGA: (*A bit blindsided.*) What?

MASHA: Arkadina, not you, dear. But one can forget!

Behind them, the sleeping MAN *has awoken.*

MASHA: So did Anton propose?

OLGA: (*A bit flustered.*) Not in so many words, but he's made clear that option is there.

MASHA: So it's in your control now?

OLGA: It's not like that. Things are just so busy with the Theatre.

MASHA: And the Theatre's managing director. (*Not without empathy.*) I understand.

OLGA: There's a history there. And it has nothing to do with my love for your brother.

MASHA: You don't need to convince me, my dear. It would help to get my mother on your side.

OLGA: Yes, she's a hard one. Does she not like actresses?

MASHA: Not just actresses, she despises the theatre.

OLGA: Nooo ....

MASHA: Oh she actively denies how much of our income comes from it.

OLGA: So what do I do?

MASHA: Try writing her a letter. Let her get to know you that way.

OLGA: Maybe I can just talk to her, gal-to-gal?

MASHA: Your troupe has already left.

OLGA: What? Oh! Why didn't you say something earlier?

MASHA: I came in and witnessed Art. And Art lives outside of time.

OLGA: (*Gathering her things.*) You're going to be late too.

MASHA: I'm ... staying.

OLGA: What? Why?

MASHA: I'm needed here.

OLGA: I was joking before, but this is just the sort of situation. I love him, but ... (*Shakes her head.*)

The formerly sleeping MAN *sits up. He breathes heavily, but the women do not hear him.*

OLGA: Can I still catch them?

MASHA: Of course. They'll hold the boat, they'll hold the tide for the famed Olga Knipper.

OLGA: (*At the door.*) Masha, if I did or said something to displease you...

MAN: (*Now approaching them.*) Hello.

MASHA *and* OLGA *scream.* OLGA *runs away.*

MASHA: Please don't hurt us! We'll give you money!

MAN: I don't want your money.

ANTON *is at the door.*

ANTON: What happened??

MAN: Masha. Do you not. Recognize me?

ANTON: Your Schmul?

MASHA: Isaak?

ANTON: Levitan???

MASHA: How are you here? Why didn't you let us know you were coming?

LEVITAN: I just. Got on the train. On impulse. And came.

LEVITAN *speaks with propulsive urgency despite his shallow breath.*

His odor now hits them. They try to appear unfazed.

MASHA: Ohhh...

ANTON: What were you thinking, man?

UNCLE NIKOLAI *is at the door, having heard the commotion.*

UNCLE NIKOLAI: Ho-ho! Should I throw this guy out?

ANTON: What? No!

MASHA: Do you want to sit, Isaak?

MARFA *is at the door, continuing with the formal attitude.*

MARFA: Dr. Chekhov, it has been over ten minutes. Is now a good time?

ANTON *and* MASHA *look at each other. There's a silent communication.*

EVGENIA: (*Appearing at the door.*) What's going on, Anton?

MASHA: Isaak Levitan has come, Mama.

EVGENIA: The Jew?

LEVITAN: Yes. The Jew.

EVGENIA *tilts her head, unimpressed, and she exits.*

LEVITAN: She's the same.

ANTON *and* MASHA *are in motion.*

ANTON: Okay, Marfa, come in.

MASHA: Isaak, why don't we get you cleaned up?

ANTON: Use my wash room, Masha. Give him my robe. Tell him about the door handle in the wash room, you have to jiggle it to exit.

MASHA: Nikolai Alexeyevich, if you'd like to wait in the garden.

UNCLE NIKOLAI: Thank you, mistress.

MASHA *ushers* LEVITAN *out.* UNCLE NIKOLAI *bows to* ANTON.

MARFA: You remember my uncle?

ANTON: Of course.

UNCLE NIKOLAI: Thank you, excellency, I have been reading not less than a few of your stories, and I enjoyed several scenes, although I do not approve of the behavior of some of your characters, but no casting of dispersions on you ...

MARFA: Uncle, I need to speak with Dr. Chekhov.

UNCLE NIKOLAI: Young lady, say 'your excellency'. I read with great jubilation that you were given the order of St. Stanislaus!

ANTON: (*Self-deprecatingly.*) Yes, third class, but no honorific is needed.

UNCLE NIKOLAI: Honorific is correct, sir, and as I am a man who cares most about what is his duty, it is not just to you that I say this, but as a mark of loyalty to my monarch, the light of Russia, and to God and all His holy angels.

A beat.

ANTON: (*Sincerely.*) Uncle Nikolai. May I call you that? Dear Marfa has become like family to us.

UNCLE NIKOLAI: (*Taking his hand, moved.*) That is one of the kindest things anyone has ever said to me—

ANTON: I understand your family is from Livadia not too far away.

UNCLE NIKOLAI: Yes, sir, your excellency.

ANTON: You'll come visit more often. Now, Marfa, what's the thing you wanted to talk to me about?

MARFA, fidgeting, is at a loss for words. So she cinches her dress from the back so it shows a slightly protruding lower abdomen.

ANTON: Oh.

MARFA: I'm sorry, sir.

UNCLE NIKOLAI: Yeah she's sorry.

MARFA: I'm sorry, uncle.

UNCLE NIKOLAI: I need to go outside.

He does. ANTON *looks at his watch, makes a judgment.*

ANTON: (*To* MARFA.) Have you had a doctor's examination yet?

MARFA: No. Is that bad?

ANTON: I'm sure it's fine. (*To* UNCLE NIKOLAI.) The camellia bushes are just starting to flower.

He closes the doors and goes to wash his hands in a basin.

ANTON: So how have you been feeling?

MARFA: Better. Kinda good now, except for the shame.

ANTON: The nausea is going away?

MARFA: Yeah. How did you know?

ANTON: It was about three months ago, yes?

MARFA: Did you hear him coming down the stairs? I told him not to go that way.

ANTON: It's okay. You look as if you're about 12 to 14 weeks.

MARFA: You're so smart.

ANTON: (*Laughs.*) It's simple science, my dear.

MARFA: I don't know anything about science. Or about anything.

ANTON: Say "ah".

MARFA: Aaaaahhhh... Would you like me take my clothes off?

She pulls up her dress, revealing her legs.

ANTON: No no, clothes are fine. "Ah".

MARFA: Aaaaahhhh...

MASHA *enters, falls effortlessly into assisting. He looks at her.*

MASHA: Isaak needed some privacy.

ANTON *returns to* MARFA.

ANTON: (*Not looking in her mouth.*) I'm not your employer right now, I'm your doctor. As your employer, I will never touch you like this. Only as your doctor. If you accept, nod your head.

She nods, stops saying "ah".

ANTON: (*To* MASHA.) Did you know about this? (*To* MARFA.) Say "ah".

MARFA: Sorry. Aaaaahhhhh....

ANTON: (*Not looking in her mouth.*) This is a free visit. Pay me back by following the advice I give you. If you want to tip me, you may say "thank you." But only once. Say "ah".

MARFA: Aaaaaaaahhhh......

ANTON: (*Checking her pulse.*) I'm just checking your pulse. Good. Say "ah".

MARFA: Aaaaaahhhhhh....

ANTON: I'm going to listen to your heart.

He puts the stethoscope to her upper chest. She stops saying "ah".

MASHA: Just relax.

ANTON: (*After a moment.*) Good. Say "ah".

MARFA: Aaaaaahhhhhh....

ANTON: (*Kneels before her, touching her abdomen and loin area.*) This might feel funny, I'm trying to see where your uterus is sitting.

MASHA: The uterus is where the baby grows. Say "ah".

MARFA: (*Tiring.*) Aaaaaahhhhh....

ANTON: It does not grow in your stomach, contrary to popular belief.

MASHA: I'll go check on Isaak.

MARFA: (*Stops saying "ah", to* MASHA.) Is he going to look in my mouth?

ANTON: No, you don't have a cold, so I have no worries about your throat. Thank you, nurse.

MASHA *exits.*

MARFA: Then why did you have me saying "Ah"??

ANTON: That was a check to see how long you'll continue to follow someone's words and not their obvious actions. Who's the boy?

MARFA: Now I feel stupid.

ANTON: No stupider than any of God's creatures. (*Standing.*) You have been in my household with morning sickness for six weeks, and I didn't notice. You have been showing for a couple weeks now: signs in the face, the hair, the nails. (*He points.*)

MARFA: Yeah! And my chest—

ANTON: Of course, and I know this, but I didn't see what was right in front of me. I didn't see one of my oldest and dearest friends lying on a bench in my yard even though I was five feet away from him.

MARFA: I mean, he just looked like a lump lying there.

ANTON: (*Not really listening.*) All because I am blinded by love for this woman, an actress who is tethered to her director in ways I stupidly thought my charm—fading though it is—would be able to sever!

MARFA: Oh, Miss Knipper is lovely. And she looks at you like—well, like they all look at you ...

ANTON: (*Stopping her.*) Marfa, who's the boy? (*Realizing.*) Is it the grocer's boy, Ivan?

She blushes. Having finished, he washes his hands.

ANTON: Speak to the boy. If he's serious...

MARFA: He's not serious. None of them are serious.

ANTON: Speak to him again. We'll put together a dowry for you.

MARFA: (*Moved.*) Oh, thank you ... your excellency.

ANTON: How is your uncle taking it?

MARFA: He said he should bash me on the head. Can you please talk to him? He won't bash me if you tell him not to.

ANTON: Yes I'll talk to him.

MARFA: Thank you, Dr. ...

A rifle shot is heard nearby, then two. A beat, MARFA *tries not to cry.*

MARFA: I hope that wasn't a cat. (*Starts to go, then turns.*) But what about my baby?

ANTON: (*Smiles.*) Your baby is a reflection of you. And you're the picture of health. (*Opens the doors.*) Uncle Nikolai, come on in.

UNCLE NIKOLAI: Yes, someone's shooting out here. (*Comes in.*)

ANTON: (*To* MARFA, *who is exiting into the house.*) Eat what you crave. No alcohol. And no Ivan, unless he comes and talks marriage with your uncle and auntie.

MARFA: Okay!!!

UNCLE NIKOLAI: Marriage. Yes yes. Good advice. I was thinking about your play we just saw. Entrancement. True entrancement. I did not approve of all the shenanigans, but one thing that stuck with me was when your character Waffles said he would stand by his wife … who had committed adultery, and yet he … (*Moved.*) He remained true to her. That takes courage. You understand.

MASHA *is at the door.* UNCLE NIKOLAI *walks outside.*

MASHA: Mama is asking for you. (*In a loud whisper.*) And did you offer that girl a dowry?

ANTON: Aren't you leaving?

MASHA: No I'm not.

ANTON: OHHHH ... Levitan came to you!

MASHA: Not like that, I made the choice before.

ANTON: Uh-huh, and where is he? He shouldn't be alone.

MASHA: He's still in the washroom.

ANTON: Right now, let's think of him as a patient, not a suitor.

MASHA: Right, because I'm such a stupid empty-headed girl I have flowers in my eyes when a boy comes around. But no, then you'd allocate money for me.

She leaves. EVGENIA *is at the door.*

EVGENIA: Well she left.

ANTON: Who?

EVGENIA: (*Sarcastically.*) Who?

ANTON: We had a house full of people.

EVGENIA: Nadia left is who. And you didn't even come say hi.

ANTON *exits.* EVGENIA *remains.*

EVGENIA: My children don't listen to their mother. They don't think that in all my time I have learned something about the way the world works. But maybe I haven't learned anything. Maybe I'm just an old fool.

ANTON: (*Having reentered.*) Are you fishing for pity in an empty room? Did you talk to Olga?

EVGENIA: The actress?

ANTON: She's very good-natured.

EVGENIA: Mmm. (*Starts to go.*) And what did you say to Marfa? She plopped herself down on the couch right next to Nadia. She's got her feet up, telling us "Oh don't mind me."

ANTON: Did you know she was pregnant?

EVGENIA: Where have you been?

She exits. UNCLE NIKOLAI *has come back.*

UNCLE NIKOLAI: I tried praying like your mother, sir, but with all this, well, maybe I don't have it right. So I'm divided. We guide them, care for them every day. But can we ever change a person's nature?

OLGA *appears at the door, blows a kiss to* ANTON, *and runs off. Was this* OLGA *or a vision? He's unsure.*

ANTON: What? Oh. Maybe.

UNCLE NIKOLAI: I know you're correct, sir, it's just that all these years we've been trying to guide this girl, but she always had an eye for the boys. And maybe it's her nature.

ANTON: People are complex.

UNCLE NIKOLAI: You see she's the daughter of my wife's sister. When she died in childbirth, we took little Marfa as our own.

ANTON: And her father?

UNCLE NIKOLAI: Well, he disowned her, because he believed that she was not his, and I have to agree; he and I, we were stationed in the Caucusus at the time when the conceiving was done, and I didn't agree with his choice, but I also could not defend her virtue, so we raised Marfa as our own, just like your Ilya Ilyich in your 'Uncle Vanya'. Waffles, right?

ANTON: Yes.

UNCLE NIKOLAI: Just like Waffles, you raise the child for the child's sake, and I'm a man of duty, and I have a question for a learned man. Is it my duty to physically punish Marfa because of what she has done? Her mother—forgive me—was a loose girl, and I felt it was a case of "spare the rod, spoil the child." Marfa was just like her mother, but my wife would not let me punish her, but now I believe that may be misguided.

ANTON: You want to beat her.

UNCLE NIKOLAI: I do not want to, but I feel it may be my duty.

ANTON: (*Takes a breath.*) My family is two generations away from serfdom, from slavery, from being mercilessly beaten with little recourse to defend themselves. My grandfather who worked like a horse to buy his freedom himself acted like a slavedriver. He beat my father so badly as a child that he had to wear a truss all his life. A year and half ago, at age 73, my father decided not to wear that truss one day, and he herniated out and died a few days later as a result. Raising us, my father beat both my older brothers so badly they were psychologically damaged, suffering from nightmares and an inability to lead stable, productive lives. I assume you were beaten.

UNCLE NIKOLAI: Yes.

ANTON: Did it make you want to act virtuously?

UNCLE NIKOLAI: Never thought of it that way, but I would say no.

ANTON: My father beat me. The difference was, the more he beat me, the more I turned to steel. (*On the edge of a threat.*) You're not going to touch that girl. (*Pulling back.*) Because, Uncle Nikolai, our family no longer operates that way. You have lived a virtuous life, not because you were beaten, but because you learned to love duty, because you sacrificed to raise a child that was not your own. You're so good, Uncle Nikolai, that you even listen to your wife's advice, and I know very few men who can say the same. (*Smiles.*)

UNCLE NIKOLAI: (*Moved, shakes* ANTON*'s hand.*) I appreciate your excellency's helping me think through this matter, and I feel very good about not laying a hand on the girl. Relieved! I will not grudge her or the baby whatsoever. (*Going to leave.*) I should say we'll send a cart around, perhaps in a week or two, to get her things. I know this is an inconvenience. It is difficult to find good help. Thank you, thank you again.

He exits.

ANTON: Oh. We are going to need a new maid. (*Upset.*) We need a new maid!

MASHA *leads in* LEVITAN. *He has wet hair, indicating he's been doused.*

ANTON: Take off your clothes.

LEVITAN: What? Why?

ANTON: I'm not going to rape you, idiot. I'm going to examine you.

LEVITAN: Antosha, your face. Is hardened towards me. Have I offended?

ANTON: Not at all.

LEVITAN: Am I still your Schmul?

ANTON: (*Softening.*) Of course.

LEVITAN: I need a minute.

MASHA: It's so ... to have you here, Isaak. I was coming to you, but now ... here you are.

LEVITAN: (*To* MASHA.) Do you have my letters? I want you to find. All my letters.

MASHA: Okay. I mean, we have trunks of letters ... but they're sorted, mostly.

LEVITAN: Find them. And bring them.

MASHA: Okay.

Thinking this might be a good sign, she exits.

ANTON: Ready?

LEVITAN: A bit longer. I have a hard-on.

ANTON: One reflex I don't have to check.

LEVITAN: How did you like. Seeing your plays?

ANTON: I'm not a theatre person. For them, it's all impulses and moods. For me, the story is the story. Tell the story the way it was intended. As a prose writer, the words don't decide. I decide. And they follow. No collaboration. No interpretation. Painting is the same, no? (*Starts examination.*)

LEVITAN: No the paint. Tells me everything. (*With lewd undertone.*) That Knipper's something. I was half asleep. When she was talking. Brother, my dream. Like Hieronymus Bosch! Bodies everywhere! My dreams Anton, my dreams. I don't know where they end. Where the real begins. It's all color, vibrant color. And this painful load. The body I lug along. Hacking and groaning. Part of me just floats. A little above. And it goads me. How serious. Are you about. Knipper?

ANTON: (*Quietly, with pride.*) It is one year I am completely monogamous.

LEVITAN: YOU?? Wow. I could. Never.

ANTON: Are you painting?

LEVITAN: I paint. It's muscle memory. I'm lost in color. The shading. The dance of light. Each painting is the last. But I go on.

ANTON: I'm going to listen to your heart now.

LEVITAN: I trust you. Sorry if I smell. (*Weeps.*) I'm dissolving.

ANTON: You're still here. (*Listens.*) You've still got that systolic murmur—fftock, fftock. A broken heart that keeps going.

LEVITAN: Thank you for hearing.

ANTON: You taught me half my craft, Isaak. To mirror nature.

LEVITAN: That's the whole craft.

ANTON: (*Listening to his lungs.*) Breathe in. And out.

LEVITAN*'s breath is shallow, and he suppresses the coughing.*

ANTON: Once more. In. And out. Okay.

LEVITAN: What's the other half?

ANTON: Mirroring people, I suppose.

LEVITAN: I avoid people.

ANTON: A lot of husbands wish that were true.

LEVITAN: Beautiful women. Are not people. They're demons. Or angels. Or both. Wrapped up in. An intoxicating package. Until you bed them. Then the magic is gone. And you might as well. Be lying. Next to your sister!

MASHA *is at the door, with a bundle of letters.*

MASHA: I've got your letters.

LEVITAN: Anton's too?

MASHA: Oh, his are more spread out... Okay. (*Goes.*)

ANTON: Bend over, Isaak, put your hands on the desk here.

He does.

ANTON: You're going to feel some pressure.

LEVITAN: OOOOOHHHHH. Are you sure? That's your finger??

They laugh, and cough.

LEVITAN: What did I say before? I can't control. What I say anymore.

ANTON: Beauty is an intoxicant.

LEVITAN: Beauty is more, Antosha. (*Weeps again.*) My whole life. I've spent. Trying to grasp it. But it won't stay. But I can't stop. I see God. He's right there. In the woman. In the tree. In the river. And I rush to catch Him. On the canvas. And I finish. And He's gone. And I'm left. With a painting. Of a tree.

ANTON: But I look at that painting and I see more than a tree.

LEVITAN: I was standing. In an oak grove. It was sunset, the light was stunning. But slipping away. No use painting. I opened my eyes wide. To soak it all in. So overwhelmed I sat down. I saw an oak leaf. On the ground. And I looked. And I saw the whole tree. Was pictured in the leaf. The tree's self-portrait. The stem was the trunk. The veins were boughs and branches. And leaves everywhere. All we do is self-portrait. I don't know whether. To rejoice or mourn.

ANTON *has washed his hands in the basin.* MASHA, *at the door, listens.*

ANTON: Well, Isaak. That microscopic terror has you by the heart. Are you right with your Maker?

LEVITAN: No. Not at all!

ANTON: (*Hesitantly.*) Three years ago. I had a hemorrhage. In Moscow, at the Hermitage. Sit down to dinner. Blood gushes up from my right lung, filling my mouth. I've always been around death, but suddenly, it had me by the throat. I'm not the mystical type, but what if with the decay of the five senses, five others were awakened? Or ninety-five? There's so much we don't know. (*A beat.*) There's this thing that happens when a story comes to me: it's like it's pressing through from another realm.

He raises up his hand as if receiving the touch of another hand in front of him.

LEVITAN: Yes. Yes!

ANTON: And it becomes urgent, like a communication from beyond.

LEVITAN: Yes. Yes.

ANTON: And it's not convenient.

LEVITAN: No.

ANTON: But reliable. There's a story always there, always ready.

LEVITAN: It screams in my head. Pull me through! I must be born! NOW!

ANTON: Maybe it's whatever is on the other side. Looking for an opening to us. Trying to let us know it's okay. Not to be afraid.

LEVITAN: Yes. That's ART. On the other side. The love of my life!

MASHA *enters, carrying bundles of letters. They turn to look at her.*

MASHA: I have the letters.

ANTON: Yes. Art.

LEVITAN: Awwww. Here I thought. It was just madness! It's a nice idea. A little dream bubble. To ponder as I slip away. (*Weeps.*)

ANTON: (*To* MASHA.) Can you give us another minute?

MASHA: Why do I always have to leave? No I'm staying. (*Sits.*)

ANTON: (*To* LEVITAN, *gently.*) Don't be afraid. I'm just a bit behind you, my friend.

LEVITAN: You! You look healthy! If I didn't know. I'd say it's all rumor. That Chekhov has tuberculosis! A rumor to magnify your name. To keep people on the edge. Of their seats. A dramatic device. To invoke sympathy! So they'll throw lavish affairs. And bring all Moscow to you!

ANTON: Come now.

LEVITAN: I don't know what's true! Everything seems suspect! Because you know. What is right here! In front of me? Pressing in? (*Mimics Anton's earlier gesture.*) DEATH! Oh! Oh, I'm going to die!! (*Starts to wail.*) I'm not ready! I haven't made right with myself!!

MASHA: Isaak, I'm here. We're here.

She and ANTON *both come closer, nearly mirroring one another's movement, and each touches* LEVITAN *on a shoulder.*

LEVITAN: (*Through sobs.*) I'm sorry. I know you're sick. I know the disease. Goes up and down. But I'm losing control. Please don't throw me out. Keep me here. These moments pass. (*Urgently, to* ANTON.) Go to Algiers. The air there. Good as medicine. And drink koumiss. It's fermented.

ANTON: I know what koumiss is.

LEVITAN: Fermented. Mare's milk. Anton, say you will. Promise.

ANTON: Okay. Koumiss. Algiers, I don't know.

LEVITAN: The disease. Takes you down. In cycles. You're better now. But it's coming back. Take time now. To heal. To build up. (*Smiles.*) Money in the bank.

ANTON: You know I could never keep money in the bank. (*To* MASHA.) Mashenka, can you get Isaak a cup of tea?

LEVITAN: I don't want anything.

ANTON *nods to her to go. She goes.*

ANTON: (*So gently.*) Isaak. The key is not to exert too much. That risks hemorrhaging a lung and a bleed out. The best scenario will be that the heart stops. On its own. And you're at peace. Sitting with someone looking at you, adoringly. (*Steps away.*) You remember that summer you asked Masha to marry you? And she said no. And she was right to do that. (*Smiling.*) I would have shot her with a gun if she had said yes, the way you shot that woodcock when we were walking.

LEVITAN: Yeah.

ANTON: Well, this is a different time. And if you ask her again... she might have a different answer.

MASHA *is at the door with tea, her hands shaking, having heard* ANTON.

ANTON: And you might have some solace in these last days.

He exits. LEVITAN *and* MASHA *are left alone.*

LEVITAN: I never got. A royalty for that.

MASHA: For?

LEVITAN: For that writer. Who shoots the seagull. Or for the rest. Of my life's tragedy. He exploited.

MASHA: Don't hold your breath.

LEVITAN: Don't hold your breath. That's a good one.

MASHA: I'm sorry, I didn't mean that.

She offers him the tea. He takes it but doesn't drink.

MASHA: Why did you come, Isaak? You're too sick to travel.

LEVITAN: I wanted to see. You Chekhovs one last time. If I made it.

MASHA: You did.

LEVITAN: When I arrived. You were all gone. But the door was open. I came in. And I felt at home. Same pictures. Same faces. Same smell. And all the memories. Of Moscow when we were young. Of Babkino. Of Melikhovo. (*Getting up.*)

MASHA: Please sit.

LEVITAN: You wrote. Anton missed the north. So I found cardboard. And painted something. For the fireplace. Haystacks in moonlight.

He has retrieved from a corner of the room a rectangular piece of cardboard with a painting on it.

MASHA: Oh. (*Taking in the painting.*) How do you do it? A masterpiece, on a piece of cardboard.

LEVITAN: Maybe not. A masterpiece. But a mantle piece.

He pushes it into the niche above the fireplace. It fits.

MASHA: Oh. It fits. Perfect.

LEVITAN: (*Looking at* MASHA.) It fits.

They are close together. She admires the painting.

MASHA: This will be in this same spot a hundred years from now.

LEVITAN: Agh. You can burn it. When I leave.

MASHA: Oh. Ohhhh. No.

He sits, pants from the exertion, ponders what to say next.

MASHA: I overheard part of your conversation with Anton. About art. And the other side. And the sublime connection that artists—true artists feel. You don't know how envious I am of you.

LEVITAN: Of me?

MASHA: Yes. And Anton, and others, who have that. I like to paint, and you've always been encouraging. But what you're describing ... it's beyond anything I've experienced. So far. I mean, I'm not that ... old that I can't experience ... new things. I can learn, if I have a teacher, a helper or something. I can be a helper too.

LEVITAN: (*Looking at the bundles of letters.*) That's a lot of letters.

MASHA: These are mine, these are some of Anton's. I was reading some of them not long ago. It gets quiet here at nighttime. And I found this funny passage you wrote—

LEVITAN: Masha.

MASHA: (*Trembling.*) Yes. Yes, Isaak.

LEVITAN: (*Pauses, breathing heavily.*) I want you. To burn. Every one. Of those letters.

MASHA: What? I can't do that.

LEVITAN: Burn them, Masha. I want nothing to remain. When I go, I go!!

He goes out quickly. MASHA *steadies herself and sits down in front of the fireplace. After a while,* ANTON *enters with a cup of tea.*

ANTON: Where is he?

MASHA *can't speak.* ANTON *comes to her, extends his hand. She takes it. He sees the painting.*

ANTON: What's this?

MASHA: (*Managing to speak.*) A gift from Levitan. For you.

ANTON: (*Looking over the painting.*) How charming! One of his haystacks in moonlight. And it fits right into the niche here. (*Sips the tea.*) Listen to that. Quiet. We haven't heard that for a month.

MASHA *rises, retrieves the bundle of her letters from Levitan and brings them to the fireplace.*

ANTON: My dear, to be fair, you're no worse off than you were a half-hour ago, when you were full of joie-de-vivre.

MASHA: Right.

ANTON: Olga slipped away without committing again. Maybe it's best. (*Shakes his head.*) Marry an actress! Maybe Mama is right. Or maybe neither of us is destined to marry. But to die virgins.

She doesn't respond.

ANTON: (*Looking around.*) So where is he?

MASHA: He ran off.

ANTON: Ran off? He's deathly ill! Which direction?

MASHA *gestures in the direction. She is seated in front of the fire looking at one of the letters.*

ANTON: We have to stop him—Marfa!!

MARFA: (*Off.*) Yes!

ANTON: Can you come here please?— (*To* MASHA.) What are you doing?

MASHA *is putting the first page of the first letter in the fire.*

MASHA: He told me to burn the letters. I assume he wants you to do the same.

ANTON: I'm not going to do that.

MARFA *is there, holding her belly.*

ANTON: (*To* MARFA.) The gentleman who was just in here, he is very ill, and he left the house in that direction. I need you to run and find him and bring him back. Don't take no for an answer, but be very gentle.

MARFA: But sir, in my condition...

ANTON: (*Impatient.*) For heaven's sake, you could run an Olympic marathon, now go!

She goes.

ANTON: (*Drily, to himself.*) And if all else fails, show him your legs.

MARFA *is back, with a letter.*

MARFA: Oh, sir, this just arrived for you.

ANTON: Thank you.

MARFA: What were you saying about my legs?

ANTON: Nothing, now go!! So much for the quiet.

MASHA *is burning the second letter. Tears are streaming down.*

ANTON: Here we go. You look like you're in a play, like Ibsen's play we saw the other night, where she burns the manuscript. (*Mocking.*) "I'm burning your child, Thea." Like anyone would just have one copy of such a precious manuscript! So contrived.

MASHA: Who's the letter from?

ANTON: (*Opening it.*) It's a note from Olga.

He smiles as he reads, but says nothing. MASHA *looks at him.*

ANTON: It's just a note.

With his hands, he tries to indicate how he doesn't want to exult while she suffers.

MASHA: Just read it.

ANTON: She says: "I talked to Nemirovich. He says, 'To the director, you are valuable. To the playwright, you are invaluable'."

MASHA: That's something.

ANTON: There's a picture, looks like a dog. Oh it must be a cow. In a wedding veil, cause it's saying "I mooooo." Like "I do."

MASHA: So someone is engaged.

ANTON: (*Glowing.*) Hardly.

MASHA *burns another letter.*

End of Act II

ACT III

April 1902. The White Dacha at Autka, Yalta. A spring morning. A parlor, a porch and a garden. A bench at some distance.

MASHA *sits in the parlor, staring at the painting on an easel.* OLGA *lies sleeping in a bed on wheels. There is a large portrait of* ANTON *hanging on the wall.*

ANTON *meanders in the garden. He uses a cane, wears a warm coat, and suppresses his cough.*

On the porch, EVGENIA *sits, waiting, dressed for church.* MUSTAFA *works, meditatively, nearby in the garden.*

MUSTAFA: You know, mother of Anton Pavlovich, prayer is of different kinds, and you don't have to wait until you are in a church or before an icon to pray with the Almighty.

She scowls and looks away.

MUSTAFA: Yes, churches and mosques are good, but nature is a great temple too, where we can worship and learn divine lessons. Right now I am cleaning out some dead leaves from last year, so new growth can come. Just so, we must let go our old habits and prejudices, if we have, so new habits can come. You see, only in nature you gain this insight, Mashallah, and not in a church surrounded by stone and smoke.

EVGENIA: Please be quiet. You are trying to lead me astray.

MUSTAFA: Not at all. Just sharing a small insight I got in the garden.

EVGENIA: That's what the serpent said to Eve.

MUSTAFA: (*Laughs.*) Yes, that's very clever—Feels like rain is coming.

EVGENIA: Nonsense. And you should have raked the old leaves months ago. You're just trying to defend your laziness.

MUSTAFA: Another thing I learned is don't pull too hard when a creature of God is clinging to the old, like a bush still holding its leaves after they are dead. You don't tug too hard, you might hurt the bush. Don't rake the bush! (*Laughs.*)

EVGENIA: What's that supposed to mean?

He is back at work. In the parlor, OLGA *is stirring.*

OLGA: (*Not awake yet.*) Anton. Where is Anton?

MASHA: Just out in the garden. He'll be here in a moment.

OLGA: (*Groans and squirms.*) I want him here now.

MASHA: Rest now, Olichka. Rest.

OLGA: Nooooo.

MASHA: It's me. Masha. It's my shift for ... 16 more minutes.

OLGA: I don't care.

MASHA: (*Feeling her head.*) You're still warm. I'm going to rub this cool washcloth on your head, okay?

OLGA: Nooooo.

OLGA *knocks over the basin of water, and she is out again.*

MASHA: Look what you did. You are a ... bit of a prima donna.

She gets down to sop up the water. ANTON *approaches the house, passes his mother, touching her shoulder.*

EVGENIA: I dreamed that Misha and Aleksander came, and the waves were right up to the garden, and I was looking for you, but you weren't there, they wanted to take me on a boat.

ANTON: I'll make sure no one takes you away, Mama.

EVGENIA: I know you will, Antosha. I know you will.

ANTON: (*Peeking in the parlor.*) Everything okay?

MASHA *grunts. He watches* OLGA.

ANTON: A sick humanity writhes and flails in wait of a true physician. (*After a beat, enters.*) Look at that monstrosity of a painting.

MASHA: Beg your pardon?

ANTON: Not yours— (*Looks at* MASHA*'s painting, jokingly.*) What is it?

MASHA: Come now. What do you think? You're always so good with offering advice to other artists.

ANTON: It appears to be our two cranes: the one with no eye, and the other one ... what's this?

MASHA: Its injured wing.

ANTON: (*Ironically.*) Ah yes, a metaphor.

MASHA: Maybe. I'm not done, I barely have the time. Any suggestions?

ANTON: Painting is not my ... (*Attention on his portrait.*) This has got to go.

MASHA: She wants it there. Is the metaphor too...? I can start over.

ANTON: Damn the critics! Paint what you want to paint. But this … at least wait until I'm dead to hang such a thing.

He takes the portrait down and hides it behind some furniture.

MASHA: She's going to complain.

ANTON: We all have some complaints, don't we. (*Going back outside.*)

MASHA: Yes we do, don't we. (*Following him out.*) Can you relieve me early? Or give either me or her something to knock us out?

ANTON: There are three bottles of morphine on the desk in my study.

MASHA *starts to go.*

ANTON: A joke.

MASHA: So can you take her?

ANTON: I'm trying to map out a floor plan for Act Three in my head. First question she'll ask is if I've made progress on the play?

EVGENIA: She's faking it.

MASHA: Mama, that's ridiculous! (*To* ANTON.) Right?

EVGENIA: I've seen a hundred girls like that. They miscarry or lose a baby, and they lay around for a month pretending to be sick. The whole household revolves around them. I'm not saying she's not in pain, but this moaning and groaning, it's grief.

ANTON: Olga has a serious infection, Mama. It's not just grief.

EVGENIA: We lost little Yevgenia, and your father would not let me grieve. May his sins be burned away in purgatory.

MASHA *unlocks the wheels on* OLGA*'s bed, jostling her.*

OLGA: Anton!

MASHA: Time to go out for some fresh air.

OLGA: No I want my husband.

MASHA *pushes the bed to the porch.*

OLGA: Ow. OW! Antoooonnnn!

ANTON: (*Giving in.*) Coming, dear!

He approaches OLGA*'s bed.* MASHA *exits.*

ANTON: How's our patient doing?

OLGA: Baaaad.

ANTON: Are you bad? Or are you "baaaaaaaad"? (*Mimicking a goat, but detachedly.*)

OLGA: I'm not "baaaaad". Just bad.

MASHA *has returned with new water in the basin and a new towel. She salutes mockingly and starts to go.*

ANTON: Masha, I'm expecting some mail today. Let's make sure the goats don't eat it.

MASHA: When have goats— ?! You know, never mind. (*Exits.*)

OLGA: What are you expecting?

ANTON: My recent test results. And the records from your procedure.

OLGA: Do you need those? You can examine me yourself.

He doesn't respond to this.

OLGA: Last night I was so bad, I was imagining if I were to go... I don't have a will. What would happen to my clothes? Who would take all my roles?

ANTON: Oh Maria Andreeva is waiting in the wings to go on.

OLGA: (*An evil look.*) I'll take you with me. (*After a beat.*) So where are you with the play?

ANTON: It's ... gestating.

OLGA: Gestating. Like a baby. (*Clutching her kidney area.*) Owwwww...

He holds her hand. EVGENIA *rolls her eyes.*

ANTON: I'm sorry it hurts.

OLGA: Make it go away.

ANTON: (*At her side.*) I'm going to hold off just a while on any more painkiller. We need you to stay awake and eat and drink as much as you can. You don't need a will, we have the fever under control. And you're from that hearty German stock: part Viking, part horse; you'll live to be ninety.

OLGA: (*Looking lovingly at him.*) Okay.

ANTON: We can give you some ointment; it'll help.

He offers her ointment.

OLGA: Can you rub it on?

EVGENIA: (*Feeling justified.*) Ahhhhh.

ANTON: Of course.

He does. Professionally.

EVGENIA: Anton, when are they coming? We're going to be late.

ANTON: They'll be here or they won't. Mama, would you come and rub this on Olga's back? I'll go see if the soup is ready.

EVGENIA: Very well.

ANTON: (*Gently mocking her judgment.*) "I was hungry and you gave Me food; I was thirsty and you gave Me drink; I was sick..."

He exits. EVGENIA *comes to* OLGA.

OLGA: Who's coming, Mama?

EVGENIA: Marfa, the maid, is coming back, with her uncle. It's been two years. She had a baby and was forced to give it up, because they couldn't afford to keep it. She would have come sooner, but she's been grieving the loss. And we need help.

OLGA: Right.

EVGENIA: Losing a child is the hardest thing a mother will ever know. I lost a baby girl. She was two years old, Little Evgenia, named after me. (*Wipes away tears.*) I didn't have time to grieve. Perhaps it was better that way. But I still grieve today.

She has finished with the ointment. OLGA *takes her hand, sincerely.*

OLGA: Sorry. I didn't know my baby. And I don't feel connected to her. I barely knew I was pregnant and I started to bleed, and just kept bleeding. I don't think I feel grief, just pain.

MASHA *and* ANTON *enter from different directions.*

MASHA: (*Whispered to* ANTON.) Look.

They look at the two holding hands. EVGENIA *turns around.*

EVGENIA: What are you looking at?

EVGENIA *stands and returns to her original seat.*

MASHA: Did Bunin and Gorky say what time they were coming today?

ANTON: I expect soon.

MASHA: Please don't do what you did yesterday and leave Olga with Mama and me, and the three of you stroll off and come back an hour later with the guts to ask me why the samovar is cold.

ANTON: You had your time to flirt with "Bouquichon" yesterday.

MASHA: I was not flirting. And so what if I was. He's a dear friend. And a support for Mama, who loves him! He was an angel for us last winter, when you were off gambling in France.

ANTON: I won 500.

MASHA: And he's a talented writer, and a wit. And exceptionally well-dressed. He's an ideal match, except for this messy divorce he's embroiled in. But Anton, I beg you not to get involved. Let this one take its own course.

EVGENIA: Are you talking about Ivan Alekseevich? Antosha, ask him if he's interested in Masha!

MASHA: Thank you, I'm asking Anton not to get involved. And you don't need to be so obvious with all your comments, okay?

EVGENIA: Masha, you're almost forty! Your window is closing!

MASHA: (*Tears starting.*) Why do you have to say it like that?

ANTON: Here we go.

EVGENIA: How should I say it?—Antosha, talk to him.

MASHA: Don't you dare!

OLGA *calls out.*

OLGA: Anton! Can you please come? I'm feeling very hot.

ANTON: (*To* MUSTAFA, *working nearby.*) Three women giving me orders, and I have a play to write. Mustafa, how do Muslim men do it with so many wives?

MUSTAFA: Only one, Dr. Chekhov. Qur'an says is best to have only one. Some men, they are greedy, but they get their reward. Allah, He rewards the people of the right and of the left. (*Eyeing* EVGENIA.)

EVGENIA: (*Not having heard.*) Why are you looking at me?

OLGA: ANTON!

ANTON: Coming. (*Stays put.*)

EVGENIA: (*To* MASHA.) Why is he looking at me?

MASHA: (*To* EVGENIA.) Leave him alone. And I beg you not to pester Bunin.

EVGENIA: (*Playfully, her hand on* MASHA*'s abdomen.*) MASHHAAAAA!!! You gotta save the eggs before the fox comes!

MASHA: What does that mean?

Bell rings.

ANTON: There's the fox!

MASHA: That might be them. Go, Anton. (*With a hint of girlish enthusiasm.*) Let me just go check my... Okay I'll be back!

She goes into the house.

OLGA: I'm HOOOOTTTTTTTT!!

ANTON: Try opening your blouse button, dear. You too Masha!

He goes off to the gate.

MUSTAFA *is once again working close to* EVGENIA.

MUSTAFA: Gracious mother of Anton Pavlovich, I just had another insight. Roses are a delightful bush, but they hold onto dead growth from last year. But I still don't rake the bush. (*Pulls out his clippers.*) NO! I clip the bush. Where to clip though—this is the mystery every gardener faces. (*Illustrating.*) Close to the dead, far from the dead. Here's wisdom: clip after the five-leaf. Five. (*Holds up his hand.*) Day of judgment has arrived, my friend. Don't rake the bush. You clip the bush!

EVGENIA: (*Sensing a scandal.*) Is that an ... innuendo? You! Is that an innuendo?

MUSTAFA: I don't know what that means.

ANTON *enters with* GORKY*, a tall man with a passionate, brusque manner, wearing a peasant's shirt.*

GORKY: I was up all night going back and forth.

ANTON: No no, your play is new and fresh. The second act is so strong. When I was reading the end, I was almost dancing with joy!

GORKY: You don't know what that—I can't...

He bends down apparently to kiss Chekhov's feet but is stopped.

ANTON: What are you doing? Stand up, man!

GORKY: Forgive me, Anton Pavlovich, that means ... But you must get your play ready for this season. My play can wait. You are still young, and you've written so much, what, in fifteen, twenty years! How many volumes does Marx have of yours? The rogue!

ANTON: My friend, I have not the time, the stamina, nor the need to fill more volumes. The virtue of youth is the fire that drives. I have this play in me. But I need to take my time.

GORKY: It's cruel. Life. That would give a man like you such a gift only to have you watch it stripped away.

ANTON: Life is not cruel, Gorky. Neither is it kind. We move, like ships, from port to port, acquiring or looting, buoyed by ambition and self-interest until we perceive we gain nothing thereby except a more heavily-laden ship, taking on water. Let it go. Let it go. Look at the birds, how they soar above us, light as the wind, looking down. They have the answer.

GORKY *is silent, shaking his head.* MASHA *has come onto the patio.*

MASHA: Good morning, Alexei Peshkov!

GORKY: Beautiful morning, Mariya Pavlovna! Brisk.

MASHA: Did Bunin not come with you?

GORKY: No, ma'am, he did not.

MASHA: Well, I trust he has a story.

GORKY: I bet he does!

MASHA: (*To* EVGENIA.) Mama, I won't be able to go to church.

EVGENIA: Why not?

MASHA: Bunin will arrive late. But Marfa and Uncle Nikolai will be here soon, and they'll go.

GORKY: (*Aside to* ANTON.) Chekhov, I don't believe Bunin will be joining us today.

ANTON: Why not?

GORKY: He caught an early train for Moscow. He said it was business related and to convey his apologies.

ANTON: Oh.

GORKY: Would you convey that? I don't want to be the bearer of bad news.

ANTON: I don't know if you know, I had a talk with him yesterday.

GORKY: Yes.

ANTON: I confronted him a bit heatedly about his intentions with my sister, who should not be made the plaything of coy suitors, or genuine, if unfortunate, married men, who leave their wives holed up in a country house while they live in the city with their common law mistresses.

GORKY: A lot of us are headed in that direction, aren't we?

ANTON: I cast no judgment, but my sister will be neither the holed-up wife nor the common law mistress.

GORKY: What was his response?

ANTON: Just saying how much he respects our family. He's a genuine soul. But I fear I've sent him on the run.

GORKY: The rest of Europe has embraced divorce, while we're still in the dark ages. This will change! Shall we perambulate?

ANTON: Yes. Let me just break the news to her. (*To* MASHA.) Masha, may I speak with you?

MASHA: I don't like the sound of that.

She sees EVGENIA *crying.*

MASHA: Mama, why are you crying?

EVGENIA: My children do not love God.

MASHA: I will go to church next week! I am just staying here to see Ivan Bunin—you know, Bouquichon.

ANTON: And, Mama, I remember all the hymns that Papa taught us.

EVGENIA: I miss your father. He never made excuses for church.

MASHA: (*To* GORKY.) Can I get you a glass of water?

GORKY: Thank you.

She exits.

ANTON: (*Just to her.*) What more can I do, Mama? I work with the sick and the poor.

EVGENIA: But your heart, Anton. What's in your deepest heart? Is God there?

ANTON: You're there. And Masha.

EVGENIA: And your siblings, including Misha.

ANTON: Sure.

EVGENIA: You're a good boy, Anton, but everyone needs to love God.

ANTON: Mama, have you forgiven him?

EVGENIA: Who?

ANTON: Father.

EVGENIA: For what?

ANTON: For what?! For breaking your heart.

EVGENIA: For what he did to me, yes. What he did to my children... Mmm ... But why do you ask? And why do you look so sad, Antosha?

ANTON: Sorry. Mama, here are two ten-ruble notes. Give one to the church, but spend the other on yourself. Don't put it in your pillow.

EVGENIA: (*Cheering up.*) Thank you, Antosha!

MASHA *has reentered with water for* GORKY. ANTON *takes her aside.*

ANTON: Apparently, Bunin left on a train to Moscow this morning.

MASHA: What? But why? ... Okay. He didn't.

ANTON: Yes.

MASHA: He didn't say why? Well, I guess I can go to church. Oh—

MARFA *enters, dragging a trunk.*

MARFA: Hello everybody.

ANTON: Welcome back.

He shakes her hand. MASHA *rebounds and redirects.*

MASHA: Marfa, you're not a moment too soon. Let's get your bags inside and we're off for church. I hope it doesn't rain.

MUSTAFA: It's going to rain.

EVGENIA: It's not going to rain.

MARFA: Uncle Nikolai told me to tell you he's been hearing all about your story about the lady and the dog, and they're saying it makes adultery seem okay, but we know how you value marriage, so he has been speaking up for you among his friends.

ANTON *smiles.*

MASHA: Wasn't your uncle going to come as well?

MARFA: He sends his apologies. He got caught up in a thornbush. (*To* GORKY.) Hello, sir.

GORKY: Hello dear sister.

ANTON: A thornbush?

MARFA: Yes. It was windy, and a gust of wind caught his newspaper and blew it into the neighbor's yard, and he went to retrieve it—he likes to read every page, so he can report it wherever he goes, and part of it—as you can imagine—went into the neighbor's thornbush and he was able to get to the page but he was not able to get himself out. I tried to help but he was worried I wouldn't get here by ten. He was certain he'd find his way out or if he didn't, a spring day spent in a thornbush is not so bad as a winter night spent in a crypt.

Varied reactions.

GORKY: Did he consider buying a new paper?

MARFA: He only has money for one paper a day, sir, ever since we lost my auntie, and with my not working for two years now. I would have come back into service earlier, but I wasn't able to get out of bed for six months after they sent my little Yulia off to the baby farm. I laughed when I first heard that name because it sounds like they pull the children right out of the earth, but instead they pull them from the clutches of such girls as me as can't raise a baby without a husband. (*Through tears.*) I apologize, I'm just so happy for Uncle Nikolai that he'll have some relief now that I'm working again. He's been carrying the whole load since my auntie passed. She did get to see my little Yulia. I whispered a prayer in her ear before they took her to protect her from evil spirits or a life on the street. And so I felt better because of that. And I feel much better these days. I still cry but it passes.

OLGA *groans in her sleep.*

MASHA: Why don't we go inside a minute? Set you up in your room.

EVGENIA: What is this? We don't need another convalescent.

MASHA: Mama please.

MASHA *walks* MARFA *inside.* MUSTAFA *goes to take the trunk.*

MUSTAFA: (*To* EVGENIA.) Rain's coming.

EVGENIA: Were you making a bawdy joke at my expense earlier?

MUSTAFA: I don't know what that means.

EVGENIA: "Don't rake the bush, clip the bush!"

MUSTAFA: You mean a sexual joke?

EVGENIA: I wouldn't use that word.

MUSTAFA: (*Shocked.*) What do you say?! How could I be so disrespectful—to myself—to the aged mother of my benevolent employer?! When I am seeking to enlighten her to the ways of God's magical world.

EVGENIA: Enlighten me? You?!

MUSTAFA: This is scandalous! I will resign unless you apologize.

EVGENIA: Apologize to you? You should apologize to me.

MUSTAFA: For insulting my character? That's it. I quit! (*To* ANTON.) Anton Pavlovich, I thank you for the trust you have put in me but I cannot work where my character is questioned.

ANTON: Your character? Who brought up your character?

MUSTAFA: (*Points at* EVGENIA.) Youuuu. Yooouuuuuuu!!!

He throws down his rake and exits into the house past MASHA, *slamming the door.*

MASHA: What's that all about?

ANTON: He quit. Mama, what did you say to him?

MASHA: And why is he going in the house? If you quit, you leave.

MASHA *and* ANTON *make eye contact.*

MASHA: THE GUN!

ANTON: No!

MASHA: We gotta get Mama out of here.

MUSTAFA *reenters hurriedly with his coat.*

MUSTAFA: Why do you look afraid? I was just getting my coat! (*To* EVGENIA.) Because it's going to rain!

He exits.

EVGENIA: Unpleasant creature.

MARFA *reenters.*

MARFA: Maria Pavlovna, there are suit cases and hat boxes in my room. Should I go somewhere else?

MASHA: I'll be right there.

MASHA *takes* MARFA *inside.*

ANTON: (*To* GORKY.) A madhouse. Let's sneak off for a walk. (*Kisses* EVGENIA.) Mama, I will see you after church. (*Leading* GORKY *off.*) I want to talk about act four, which seems a bit tacked on. You've got your strongest characters having left the stage...

EVGENIA *is alone. Distant thunder.*

MASHA *enters with* MARFA.

MASHA: We need to go or else we'll get caught in the rain. Mama, do you have your kerchief? Of course you do. Okay. (*Sees* OLGA.) Where's Anton? ANTOOONNNNN!!! He did it. He did what I explicitly told him not to do. (*To* MARFA.) Take Mama, I have to stay with my sister-in-law. (*To* EVGENIA.) Come on, Mama, Marfa is going to take you.

EVGENIA: My children.

MASHA: Yes, your children! (*Swallows anger, to* MARFA.) You remember, the church is only a half mile, not even, but there's some uneven ground about halfway so hold her hand.

IVAN, *the grocer boy from ACT I, has entered and he tries to quietly call* MARFA. *Everyone notices.*

IVAN: (*In a whispering call.*) Marfa! Marfa!

MARFA *hears him and turns away.*

IVAN: Marfa, I'm sorry. I said I'm sorry.

MARFA: (*Coming towards him.*) Go away, Ivan!

IVAN: I saw you walk by the store and I had to come. Why don't you answer my letters? Why won't you talk to me?

MARFA *ignores him, but doesn't walk away.*

IVAN: My father was the one who said no. I was ready. He has me watching the store day and night. He's okay with you, but he doesn't want a baby hanging around, driving customers away.

MARFA: Sorry for the inconvenience.

IVAN: You're talking to me now. So if we were to get together, do you think your boss would offer the dowry still?

MARFA: Ivan, why are you bothering me??

IVAN: Why are you mad? We could use that to set up somewhere so I don't have to be a serf for my father.

MARFA: I need to go.

IVAN: Will you answer my letters? Please?

MARFA: Yes, but you have to go.

IVAN: Okay I'll go. I'll go!

MARFA: I'm sorry, Mistress. What were you saying about the walk?

MASHA: Just hold her hand when it's rocky.

MARFA: I'll treat her like she's my own mother.

MARFA *and* EVGENIA *exit. Thunder, a bit closer.* MASHA *returns to the patio, decides to move* OLGA.

MASHA: Olga, I'm going to move you back inside in case it rains.

She moves the bed, over some bumps back into the parlor.

OLGA: OW!

MASHA: Sorry.

OLGA *sits up, looks around.* MASHA *looks out at the sky.*

OLGA: I'm hungry.

MASHA: Mariushka is making some soup for you.

OLGA: Where's my Anton?

MASHA: He's in the garden with Gorky.

OLGA: Thank you, I meant the painting.

MASHA: He took it down.

OLGA: But I want it here.

MASHA: (*Imitating.*) "But I want it here."

OLGA: Is it too much for me to ask help decorate the house? I'm the WIFE of the man who owns it.

MASHA: Take it up with the MAN.

OLGA: Masha, come back here. You can't simply walk away when we're having a discussion.

MASHA: This is turning into a fight. And in the Chekhov household, we do not fight.

OLGA: Right, in the Chekhov household, you avoid! You make a smarmy comment and change the subject or leave the room, as if your wit can keep you from having to deal with the issue.

MASHA: I feel I'm being sucked into one of your dramas.

OLGA: I am a part of this family now, but you and your mother and your brother are not letting me be.

MASHA: We've been waiting on you for weeks, restoring you to health.

OLGA: So you can send me back to Moscow.

MASHA: Olga, you and I live in Moscow! This is Yalta, where Anton lives.

OLGA: In a house you designed.

MASHA: I sketched the idea.

OLGA: You and Anton decorated the whole thing. If you want to put a vase of flowers on the table, you do it.

MASHA: Put flowers wherever you want.

OLGA: This is the family's center. I should feel at home here.

MASHA: You seem very much at home.

OLGA: I feel like a guest that has overstayed my welcome. I see the way you treat Ivan Bunin—"Oh Bouquichon, Bouquichon!" He could puke on the floor, and you would put a frame around it.

MASHA: So you're jealous. What is enough to satisfy you?

OLGA: I want your trust. And none of you will give it to me—I mean, I expected it from my mother-in-law, but you are my friend. And Anton—sometimes he gets that little smile, and he's a thousand miles way, flying on a sled to Sakhalin.

MASHA: I don't know what to tell you. Friend. That's the nature of the man. And of the man's family you married into. And didn't invite me—your friend!—or your mother-in-law to the wedding!

OLGA: His idea! And it was all wrapped up in that trip to the spa with the koumiss—his choice!

MASHA: Sure. But we don't stay mad at him. He's the best functioning man in this family. He provides for all of us—not just the family, HUNDREDS of others. You, you're the decadent actress who went and eloped with him. And then instead of giving birth, you create a drama with yourself at the center!

OLGA: Oh, this is my fault?!

MASHA *exits. A crash is heard in the kitchen, like soup bowls dropping and breaking on the floor, along with a woman's cry.* OLGA *does a silent scream.*

MASHA: (*Off.*) What in the name of —??

OLGA: (*After a moment, more calmly.*) Was that my soup?

MASHA *reenters, soup on her apron. A beat.*

MASHA: This is what happens when Chekhovs fight. (*With empathy.*) I know you're upset about losing the baby.

OLGA: Right now I'm just hungry. Even for Mariuhska's borscht.

MASHA: It's pretty much all she can make anymore. So we let her. We're not the Prozorovs. I'll see if she has more.

She exits towards the kitchen.

ANTON *and* GORKY *are in the garden.*

GORKY: Forgive me, Anton Pavlovich, there is no way that a lump of coal like myself can give you a critique. But I can say when I see your plays, I am always swept into a storm of emotion, but I don't leave with hope.

ANTON: (*Glibly.*) Can I give away what I don't have myself?

GORKY: More importantly, I don't leave with vision.

ANTON: The vision is "look at your lives, how deplorable they are."

GORKY: What about the future?

ANTON: I usually put a passage in there talking about two hundred years from now, what will they remember?

GORKY: I mean the sense that we can do something here, today for the future. A vision to feel part of something, a movement.

ANTON: And the censors? That can land you in prison—as you know!

GORKY: You brought me here, sat me down, engaged me in this ritual. You immersed me in these stories, whipped up my feelings, and now I want a glimpse of why, so I can bend and change, reform. I'm penitent now, I see how absurd our lives are, but I want something different. I want transformation.

ANTON: You want church.

GORKY: But the communion at church, the transformational moment. I want a glimpse of the eternal and my place in it!

MASHA *brings soup to* OLGA.

ANTON: But who feels that at church anymore?

GORKY: The more reason the theatre must fill in the gap!—What, what's that look?

ANTON: I should put a character like you in my next play.

GORKY: Anton Pavlovich, I thought we were friends.

ANTON: No, not to lampoon you. (*A beat.*) When I write a story, I knock—(*taps twice.*)—come inside and sit with you as a character, breathe your air, drink your tea, hear your troubles and see how you're vexed with the same basic problem of life as all. And you want to get out of your own way but you can't, but somehow because I'm sitting here with you, because we share a story and a laugh, because I take this time to feel with you, something rises, some little puff of pure incense, some clue to the ancient mystery … I think empathy is the best I have been able to offer.

GORKY: Well, what else could we ask from you?

ANTON: (*Thinks.*) Love.

GORKY: They're the same, no?

OLGA: ANTON!

ANTON *looks over towards her.*

GORKY: Do you … ?

ANTON *shakes his head.*

GORKY: (*After a moment.*) How is your play coming?

ANTON: I have another story trying to push its way in.

GORKY: What's the story?

ANTON: (*Smiles, moved.*) A country doctor and his pretty young wife are trying to have a child, but she miscarries. Do you know what an ectopic pregnancy is?

GORKY *shakes his head.*

ANTON: It can be fatal. It's when the embryo settles not in the womb but in the fallopian tube. Anyway, this country doctor suspects his wife--whom he adores--has had an ectopic pregnancy.

GORKY: Does she die?

ANTON: Oh she lives. It's just— (*Looks deeply at* GORKY.) There's a clear window of time when an ectopic terminates, 8 to 12 weeks. 8 to 12 weeks keeps going through the head of this country doctor ...

GORKY: (*Quickly, as if solving a riddle.*) He was traveling in the provinces when she got pregnant!

ANTON: Something like that.

GORKY: So she cheated.

ANTON: He doesn't know, but he suspects. And he doesn't know what to say to her, or how to be around her. It might not have been ectopic, and he'll never know.

GORKY: Oh. (*A beat.*) You should have her die.

OLGA: ANTOOOOONNNNNN!!

ANTON: (*To* OLGA.) Be right there! (*To* GORKY.) Gorky, you'd make a better advocate than judge. But I'm going to think about this discussion, and it's going to help me with my play.

ANTON *goes to the house.* GORKY *starts writing in his notebook.*

ANTON: How is the patient feeling? Are we fattening you up yet?

OLGA: On Mariushka's borscht? I can barely keep it down.

ANTON: Do one of your acting exercises: imagine it tastes delicious.

OLGA: That's an idea. (*Closes her eyes, tries it, smiles big, then gags.*) No. Doesn't work.

ANTON: Keep at it.

MASHA: (*Enters, with bread.*) Here's some bread to help it go down.

ANTON *starts to head back out.*

OLGA: Stop. Where's the painting?

ANTON: Your icon of Saint Anthony? I burned it, as a work of heresy.

OLGA: I want it back! (*Bites some bread. to* MASHA:) Oh you sweetheart, you put butter on it.

ANTON *starts to head back out.* MASHA *stops him on the patio.*

MASHA: Anton, where are you going? Bring Gorky in the parlor.

ANTON: We're discussing art.

MASHA: We're all artists here!! Why don't you see that? Include us.

ANTON: Sorry.

MASHA: You keep running away. Go be with your wife. She needs you.

ANTON: Masha, I have reasons for what I do.

MASHA: And you have a way of detaching.

ANTON: I'm not detaching from Olga.

MASHA: What then?

ANTON: Masha, do you trust me?

MASHA: Trust? Sure.

ANTON: Okay then.

MASHA: Did Gorky say why Bunin had to go?

ANTON: Uhh ... he didn't know exactly what happened.

MASHA: Okay.

She goes back into the parlor.

OLGA: Mashenka, I need to use the wash room. Could you help me?

MASHA: Sure.

She helps OLGA *out of bed and helps her offstage. Thunder.*

ANTON: Alexei Peshkov, come to the porch, it looks like rain.

ANTON *and* GORKY *sit at the table on the porch.*

ANTON: What were you writing?

GORKY: (*Bursting.*) A hundred, two hundred years from now, will they remember us? Yes. I will act, I will not lay down, I WILL be remembered.

ANTON: Your eternity will not be found in people remembering you.

GORKY: You don't think people will remember you!

ANTON: Seven years. Okay, seven and a half. But these people you're talking about—a hundred, two hundred years from now—they may speak about you, but do they care about us? Right now, if you're sitting with someone who doesn't care about you, you get up and leave the room.

GORKY: They will still care about you, because of how your words make them feel.

ANTON: I've known fame, my young friend—it's a minefield we mistake for a gold mine.

GORKY: It's a fact they will remember you. So... how do you WILL to be remembered? As a doctor of the poor? As a builder of schools? Or as a writer?

ANTON: I don't know.

GORKY: You're compiling your 'Complete Works', how can you not know?

ANTON: (*Ironically.*) Maybe I'll be remembered as a radical now I'm publishing my stories in your leftist journals.

GORKY: For 'In the Ravine'—(*Laughs.*) As much as I liked it. If you had written what is actually happening in that village ...

ANTON: Drunken syphilitic children are not the stuff of art.

GORKY: Those drunken syphilitic children are the reality. Their torment, the oppression they face is a direct result of the tyranny of our country's governance. If your empathy takes you far enough to feel for the people, to care about them in their misery, take one more step and love them. And if you love them, you will fight for them. Proclaim to the world the truth of their plight. (*With boylike enthusiasm.*) Oh I love our talks. I get such great ideas talking to you.

ANTON: (*Laughing.*) Yes I'm definitely going to have that character in my new play. And I'll tell you what, it will deal with class too.

GORKY: I'll publish it! In 'Knowledge', our journal.

ANTON: Are you quite serious?

GORKY: What's the play called?

ANTON: 'The Cherry Orchard.'

GORKY: We'll give you 4500 rubles for first periodical rights. Before Adolf Marx gets his hands on it.

ANTON: Deal.

They shake.

ANTON: So how do you want to be remembered as a writer?

GORKY: Burn it all. I don't care to be remembered as a writer.

ANTON: What then?

GORKY: I want to start a revolution.

ANTON *hesitates, then laughs.* MASHA *and* OLGA *have reentered. Lightning and thunder.*

MASHA: Gentlemen, join us in the parlor?

They come into the parlor. ANTON *helps* OLGA *back onto the bed.*

OLGA: Thank you.

MASHA: So what have you been conspiring about?

ANTON: Art.

GORKY: Revolution.

They laugh.

GORKY: I was just about to encourage Anton to turn things upside down in his new play. Put the poor people center stage, not to the side the way you have a nanny or a footman—and not just in comedy either. All these bourgeois stories we see on stage are modeled on Turgenev at best and, for the most part, the French melodrama—

OLGA: Don't underestimate melodrama to hold an audience!

GORKY: Well, they keep up the idolatry of the wealthy and the intelligentsia. I say put the people on stage in all their grubby splendor.

ANTON: The theatre is still an art of rhetoric, and the people—my visionary friend—are about as articulate as a cabbage being chopped into cole slaw.

GORKY: In your short stories, you animate EVERYONE. Just try putting those folks on stage. This maid of yours, she's got a story. And that gardener!

MASHA: Don't remind me! I thought we were going to witness a murder.

OLGA: So this is nice, but where's Bunin?

MASHA: Apparently, he got on a train.

OLGA: Noooo... This wouldn't have anything to do with the talk you had with him yesterday, would it, Anton?

MASHA: What talk?

OLGA: I saw them in the yard, and I saw Antosha wagging his finger like this— (*Gestures.*) And I thought what a great gesture for a play ... but it could have been the morphine. (*Laughs.*)

The rain starts.

MASHA: (*Seething.*) What was this talk about, Anton?

ANTON: Maybe not in front of everybody, Masha.

GORKY: Here comes the rain.

MASHA *takes* ANTON *aside.*

OLGA: (*To* GORKY.) What did I say?

MASHA: (*To* ANTON*, trying to keep tone down.*) I told you not to get involved. I told you to let this one go at its own pace. Apparently, you just want me to be the spinster caretaker for your home and your affairs.

ANTON: That's not it.

MASHA: Then why do you continue to get in the way of my happiness? Because you're only letting the perfect man through for me? There's no such thing! I'm just looking for a caring person that I can spend my days with, that I can open my heart to.

ANTON: It's a world of men who burn through women like they're cigars. Bunin is a good person, but he's married, Masha.

Levitan—rest his soul—was a sublime artist, but a reckless human being. Look at your siblings, look at the messes their marriages are in, look at Mama and Papa, look at ME!

MASHA: You've already given up on Olga?

ANTON: No. I love Olga. But marriage will just break your heart.

MASHA: Listen. You might have abandoned hope in marriage and this world, but don't drag me down with you. This woman in there is an actress at the peak of her career, and she almost died trying to give life to your progeny. What is that look? I have half a mind to pack a bag and chase after Bunin and just be his mistress since marriage is such a heartbreak!

She exits. The rain starts coming down harder.

ANTON *goes into a coughing bout.* GORKY *puts his arm around him.*

GORKY: You okay, Doc?

ANTON: Yes. Oh, Gorky, the problem with revolutions—and other victories... (*Looks at* OLGA.) ... is sometimes they succeed.

GORKY: That's a problem?

ANTON: (*Back to* GORKY.) There's a celebration. Then you become what you hated.

A beat.

GORKY: Oh, Chekhov, you're too philosophical for your own good.

Commotion from offstage as MARFA *and* EVGENIA *run in screaming and laughing from the rain. They are followed by* IVAN. MASHA *opens the door to the kitchen.*

MASHA: What's going on?? Mama, are you okay?

EVGENIA: Fine! Just got a little wet! (*Laughs.*)

MARFA: (*Winded from the run.*) Ohhhh, we were almost halfway! And we saw the storm coming. We turned and headed this way as fast as we could. Your mother was faster than me! We saw Ivan and he said he had to deliver something to the house.

MASHA: Well come on in and dry off! There's some soup.

MASHA, MARFA, EVGENIA *and* GORKY *go off towards the kitchen.*

IVAN *goes to hand* ANTON *a large envelope.*

IVAN: Here, Dr. Chekhov. It says on the envelope it's important and fragile, so I hid it inside my shirt when the rain started.

ANTON: Thank you.

IVAN: I want you to know, I was not happy the way things went with Marfa. And turning away the baby. That was my father, not me.

ANTON: Okay. Why don't you get some soup?

IVAN *exits into the kitchen.* ANTON *pulls two separate reports out of the envelope. He looks one over.*

OLGA: What are those?

ANTON: These are medical reports. This one... (*Indicates the one he's reading.*) ... is for me in my recent check.

OLGA: What does it say? Anton? Don't keep this from me.

ANTON: (*Deflecting.*) Nothing we didn't already know, or at least didn't suspect. Disappointing ... The other is yours from your surgery. (*Looking that one over.*) Olga. It's curious, the timing. My mother's right. Usually, a miscarriage is a quicker encounter. The woman may experience pain, but nothing like what you're going through. Did your surgeon mention the possibility of an ectopic pregnancy?

OLGA: I don't know. They chloroformed me, and I was out, and I've been doped up or in awful pain since. What does it say there?

ANTON: Just what they did, no diagnosis. And the date, March 31st. An ectopic is … well, the complications look a lot like what you're going through.

OLGA: Maybe that's it. Would that affect me having another baby?

ANTON: Yes, it reduces your chances. About half.

OLGA: Well, that's still something. We can keep trying.

ANTON: Yes. Yes. So what's your guess of the date you got pregnant?

OLGA: Well, we were only together in late February—otherwise it would have been what, October?

ANTON: Right.

He sits.

OLGA: Are you okay? We will keep trying, Anton. Look at me, we will keep trying.

He doesn't look at her, but stays at some distance. MASHA *enters.*

MASHA: Olichka, why don't you come into the other room? We'll give Anton time to consider— What's wrong? Olga?

MASHA *looks at* ANTON.

MASHA: What is it?

ANTON: My ... medical report.

Silence. MASHA *looks at the report, shakes her head, starts to well up.*

ANTON: (*Suddenly, as if a discovery.*) She's lost her baby. Of course! She's lost her ... Ooohhh! (*Moved.*)

MASHA: (*Looking at* OLGA.) Of course. Are you just absorbing that ...?

ANTON: My character, in 'The Cherry Orchard': Liubov. She's lost her baby, a son. Precious. He drowned in the river ... when the tutor wasn't looking. But she can't blame the tutor. No. She wants to, but she blames herself and her own ... infidelity. Her past, her sins weigh heavily on her, and she can't seem to burn them away, no matter how much she gives, or loves. Grief and guilt, grief and guilt. How sad—Oh I've got to write this down. This is the tone that vibrates through the play. The loss of a precious trust. And it's your own fault.

He exits. OLGA *and* MASHA *exchange looks.*

End of Act III

ACT IV

Yalta, April 1904. The setting is the same as Act 3, but indoors. It's sunset.

MASHA *and* OLGA *sit on a sofa with Anton's will.*

MASHA: I can't look. (*A beat.*) I can't look.

OLGA: I'll look.

MASHA: Okay.

OLGA *takes it, breathes.*

MASHA: Wait. You said it's addressed to me.

OLGA: Yes.

MASHA: But he entrusted it to you.

OLGA: Right.

MASHA: That's a good sign.

OLGA: Okay.

MASHA: Because he included us both in that … so he's thinking of both of us. Okay I'm ready.

OLGA: Okay. But I just want to say …

ANTON *enters, looking not unlike a ghost. His struggle with TB is at a similar stage to Levitan in Act 2, with less exhaustion and panic.*

ANTON: Boo.

They scream.

MASHA: ANTON!

ANTON: What are you two. Conspiring about?

MASHA: Nothing.

ANTON: What are you hiding?

MASHA: Nothing, would you leave us?

OLGA: It's your will.

ANTON: Oh.

MASHA: We should wait. This is premature.

OLGA: Yes, he's going to live a long life.

ANTON: Should I leave?

MASHA: Yes.

OLGA: Thank you.

He shuffles out, but just past the door.

OLGA: You're still there, aren't you?

ANTON: For heaven's sake.

He shuffles away.

OLGA: I have to say before we do this, I know the past few years have been up and down ... And our friendship, despite the terrible upstaging of Anton's celebrity, I hope it was founded on sincere affection and not just convenience. I hope it is still strong and ever remains that way.

MASHA *says nothing.*

OLGA: I care for you, Masha. You're like a sister; a bit hard to read, but tender.

MASHA: I was a bit starstruck at first. With you. The illusion of a person precedes the reality, like seeing a Bedouin coming into view across a hazy desert. Your style has more flair than I'd been accustomed to. This sophisticated, Bohemian life you lived—I was both dazzled and aghast. What I appreciate is your forthrightness, which sometimes I took as brash, but now I see as earnest.

A beat.

MASHA: Whatever it says here, we have to be strong.

OLGA: Masha, I have my own money.

MASHA: Can I ask something? Sincerely. Marriage is a complex thing. At different times, I considered marrying for protection, for pity, for money, for status, for children, or just to shut up the family. Why did you marry Anton?

OLGA: Love. I loved him. Love him. I have my own money. I have my own fame. I have my own issues—

MASHA: What will you do?

OLGA: I'll go back to the world I know. Costumes, the smell of grease paint, reading reviews and cursing the reviewers.

MASHA: Will you marry again?

OLGA: I don't think so. What will you do?

MASHA: Well, if he leaves me anything substantial in here ...

OLGA: He will.

MASHA: Well then, I will probably stop teaching. I hope to paint. And ... we have created a home here, Mama and me. There's so much to do always, people coming, people calling, it's like a shrine here for every Russian who worships their God through art rather than religion. I don't know that that will abate if he passes. So I've been thinking someone needs to see to this place. And to Mama. Maybe it will become a museum.

OLGA: To Anton? Forgive me, Masha, but you don't need to serve him any more. Be the star of your own show: paint, travel, have affairs with mysterious foreign men!

MASHA *laughs.*

OLGA: I mean it, you don't need to be under his shadow anymore.

MASHA: Part of me agrees with you. Part of me feels this has been more of a partnership, a family business. All that work, all the struggle could just vanish within a decade, all that brilliant art—that I know I'll never be able to match if I live to a hundred.

OLGA: You don't know that.

MASHA: Olga, it's okay, I know I'm not a remarkable talent. And so maybe this is how I can impact the world, if not through my own art. We can keep his papers, and his things, and they can inspire the next generation. We just keep the door open.

OLGA: You know it's more than that. What about marriage?

MASHA: I'll keep the door open for that too.

OLGA: What I'm afraid of is that you could take this on, out of a sense of obligation in your usual long-suffering Masha way, and down the road you find you're not happy, and you become resentful of Anton for once again sucking you into doing what he needs and not what you want, but now it's too late because you're ... fifty-five.

MASHA: That's not that old.

OLGA: For a man!

They laugh. This is a 'Seagull' reference.

MASHA: I hear you. And traveling does sound nice.

They embrace. Laughter and tears.

ANTON: (*Just off.*) I can just tell you. What's in the will.

MASHA: Antosha!!!

ANTON: (*Coming in.*) I feel like Solomon. Dividing the baby. Except I'm the baby too. Olga, you get five thousand. And the Gurzuf cabin. The siblings get a little. Masha, you get the house. The bank account. The royalties. It's all yours. Now I have to go. To the lavatory.

He shuffles off. They absorb what they've heard. MASHA *is moved, quiet.* OLGA *is mildly shocked and lets go a milder version of the silent scream we saw in Act 3.* MARFA *enters.*

MARFA: Excuse me, mistress, mistresses. Uncle Nikolai is asking about how he should refer to Dr. Chekhov. He read in the paper that Dr. Chekhov gave up his position, in a "protest" I think they call it for that striking gentleman who was here, "Borky" was it? Anyway, should he call him "excellency" still since it was his choice—I seem to have walked in on something, I'm sorry, I guess I'll just tell him to call him whatever he wants. Okay.

MARFA *exits. The spell is broken.* OLGA *exhales, kisses* MASHA *on the cheek and exits into the kitchen.*

MASHA *sits and looks around at the house, now hers. She will be here for 53 more years. She flips through the will to the final page.*

MASHA: (*Moved, reads.*) "Help the poor. Look after mother. All of you live in peace."

ANTON *shuffles back in.*

ANTON: We have to get. That door handle fixed. On the flush toilet.

MASHA: Anton. I just want to thank you. Sincerely.

ANTON: (*Sitting next to her.*) You had doubts, Mashenka?

MASHA: (*On verge of tears.*) No. Well...

ANTON: Who else is there? We did it. Together. (*After a quick beat.*) What correspondence?

MASHA: (*Happy for the redirection.*) I'm handling it. There is one issue. Marx is demanding the proofs for 'The Cherry Orchard,' but the censor is still blocking Gorky from publishing it. If you send the proofs, Marx will rush to print, Gorky will be stuck with no one to buy his.

ANTON: (*Considers a moment.*) We've stalled. As long as we can. The proofs. Are on my desk. Send them to Marx. Wire Gorky to send. The full 4500.

MASHA: But that will bankrupt their paper.

ANTON: (*Stirred up.*) Do you think. I do this. For me? (*Trying to calm himself.*) I can't get worked up. He'll survive. (*Hearing laughter from the kitchen.*) I need your help. Until they leave.

MASHA: Okay.

She gets up and goes out. He's alone for a bit.

ANTON: I didn't say. I wanted. To be alone.

The door opens. It's NEMIROVICH.

NEMIROVICH: Anton.

ANTON: Oh Nemirovich. Please come.

NEMIROVICH: Not here to praise you. After seeing the local Yalta production of 'The Cherry Orchard' today, I'm ready to write a scathing review scolding the writer for wasting my time.

ANTON: As am I.

NEMIROVICH: Was it painful to watch it? You squirm when you see us do it.

ANTON: The good thing. About being at death's door. You can excuse yourself. People don't take offense.

OLGA *comes in quietly, sits beside* ANTON.

NEMIROVICH: I want to talk about your play.

ANTON: I've apologized.

NEMIROVICH: We haven't found the balance yet in our production. 'The Cherry Orchard' is intricate. It's like lace.

OLGA: I think it's like 'The Seagull.' everyone's in love with someone they can't have—

ANTON *nods along, not disagreeing.*

NEMIROVICH: But it's more subtle than 'The Seagull'.

ANTON: Well. My libido too. (*Gestures.*)

NEMIROVICH *laughs,* OLGA *doesn't.*

NEMIROVICH: I've been thinking about the alternation between what seems like Naturalism and Farce and the Maeterlinck Symbolism. It's a hard combination, Anton—Yeah, you act like it's so simple, and why don't we just get it, but it's not. And I was thinking about why there's such a mystical feeling...

ANTON: Please.

NEMIROVICH: I am not flattering. I'm trying to understand these plays. Come war come revolution, we'll be running them a long time. Touring not just the country, but the world. Stanislavski and I have plans, but we're not there yet with your plays. The base you have is the Real and the heartfelt, which you break with moments of absurdity—like the Vagrant coming in, or Lopakhin saying "moooo". These jolt us out of the emotion and make us question what's the real perspective on these things. It's not that pain isn't there. It's that we can't trust it, shouldn't hold onto it. That right next to that pain is always joy, and that, with the particular alternation you use, the Sublime arises, and I don't know that you do it fully consciously, it's an instinct. I was talking to Andrei Bely, and he called the effect "an opening into eternity."

OLGA: I know you couldn't see it, my love, but that audience was so moved by the play today.

MARFA *enters with* ANTON*'s pince-nez.*

MARFA: Here you are, sir.

ANTON: Oh thank you. (*To* OLGA.) Nostalgia. Is like opium. Let's keep our eye. On the future.

OLGA: Well said well said.

MARFA: Sorry, has anyone seen Uncle Nikolai?

OLGA: No.

NEMIROVICH: (*Amused.*) Is he the one who wants to catch a ride with us? He said he'd ride next to the driver and would jump off so we wouldn't have to slow down the carriage.

ANTON: Maybe he went. For a walk. He likes the outdoors.

MARFA *goes to exit, but is brought back in by* MASHA *and* EVGENIA *tiptoeing in.* IVAN *enters as well, stands behind* MARFA.

NEMIROVICH: This infamous pince-nez of his! That he always loses somewhere. And someone has to send it on the next train, and until then he's blind. Olga told me, she said one eye is nearsighted and the other is farsighted, and I've never heard of anything like that. But it makes so much sense. With one, he sees up close and personal, with feeling. And the other is set back, analytical, a little hard even.

ANTON: I'm a doctor. Was a doctor. Now I'm a corpse.

No one laughs.

NEMIROVICH: The perfect doctor: diagnostic distance and an empathetic touch.

ANTON: (*Disturbed.*) Nemirovich, stop. You don't know. My burden.

NEMIROVICH: It's just about the plays, my friend. (*To others.*) How to perform them. When you act in comedy, you play into the laughter, lean in; in drama, you push the feeling, more tears, more rage, to get more response!

NEMIROVICH *rises and moves downstage, as if trying to envision the idea he's articulating, as if he's trying to see the audience. He uses a gesture reminiscent of the hand pressing from Anton and Levitan's scene in Act 2.*

NEMIROVICH: (cont'd) In this new theatre, you connect to the audience, you know they're there, but the way, in mindful moments, we are aware of the angels, or the spirit world, or the ancestors ... We don't manipulate the angels, we are edified by them. If we're mocking someone, we feel their reprimand, and we remember our own fault or vulnerability. And when we are despairing, we gain perspective from their eyes, that in life, even pain is a gift, because humanity is a blip of consciousness in the universal experience of oblivion. And in that thought, we sigh and separate from our pain. We see ourselves a speck of dust caught in the moon light shining through a window and then gone from sight.

A silence. ANTON *struggles to respond. Someone passes gas. Everyone turns to* IVAN.

MARFA: Ivan!

IVAN: Oh. Sorry.

Attention goes back to ANTON.

ANTON: I just wanted. To write. A comedy. But what you said. Sounds good.

OLGA: We gotta go. Got a train to catch.

NEMIROVICH *shakes* ANTON*'s hand.* ANTON *holds onto it, and takes* OLGA*'s hand.*

ANTON: Thank you. All is forgiven. All is forgiven.

Stunned, NEMIROVICH *keeps his composure until he gets outside.* OLGA *embraces* ANTON *so hard he winces.*

OLGA: You're coming in three weeks. Write me every day. Even if it's just one word.

Hugs and tears are exchanged as they go. ANTON *calms himself.*

MASHA: I'll see you to the gate.

When they leave, EVGENIA, MARFA, *and* IVAN *exit towards the kitchen.*

MARFA: (*To* EVGENIA.) That was so moving. Did you understand what he said?

EVGENIA: Not a word.

MARFA: Me neither, but it was still moving. Have you seen my uncle?

IVAN: He walked home.

They go. ANTON *leans back in his bed.* MASHA *reenters. She turns the lights down, draws the curtains.*

MASHA: "All is forgiven"—what did you mean by that?

ANTON: (*Dismissively.*) Oh.

MASHA: What happened?

ANTON: One way. Or another. We all pay. For our sins. So why not forgive? (*Emotional.*) And now. I'm spent.

MASHA: (*Sits, holds his hand.*) All is forgiven.

A beat. OLGA *reenters, goes to the painting of* ANTON, *takes it down, throws her shawl around it, goes to the door with it, blows a kiss and exits.*

MASHA: (*Still holding his hand.*) What did you think of Nemirovich's ideas about your writing?

ANTON: I don't. Listen. To flattery.

MASHA: Your work will live on.

ANTON: (*Squirming.*) Masha please.

MASHA: Okay okay. You rest now, Antosha. Rest.

She pats his hand and exits. ANTON *is left lying on the bed. He breathes heavily, and coughs some.*

Quiet. A cough. Two coughs, three. Quiet. A pounding is heard off. And a voice. Increasingly frantic.

UNCLE NIKOLAI: (*Muffled, off.*) Help. Help! Heeeeellppp!!

ANTON *opens his eyes.*

ANTON: Masha? Mashaaaa??

MASHA *enters.* ANTON *points in the direction of the voice, and she goes. A moment later, the pounding stops. Then,* UNCLE NIKOLAI *enters, flustered and embarrassed.*

UNCLE NIKOLAI: (*Off.*) Thank you so much, thank you. (*Entering.*) Your excellency—forgive me, Anton Pav … Dr. Chekh-, I was uncertain how to get out … I have never tried a flush toilet before. Quite miraculous actually, the way the water just whissshooo—, and everything was fine until I wasn't able to get out, not sure what kind of door handle you have there, and in my haste, I may have knocked over a candle. And then it was dark, and well, sir, you know I do get a tad claustrophobic. Well now it seems everyone has left and I am not certain where to go.

MASHA: They just left.

UNCLE NIKOLAI: (*Heads for the door.*) Well, that's something, I was hoping to catch a ride, but no matter, God leads the way. Isn't it so, your excellency? Where would be without God leading us? Take a step, and He …

He fiddles with the door, perhaps pulling when he should push.

UNCLE NIKOLAI: Oh. Every door has its personality in this house. God keep you. I will pray for you. And thank you for your services to His Majesty's dominion. Order of Stanislaus or not, you have served your fellow people of this country, and we gratefully thank you. (*To* MASHA.) And thank you. Thank you for ... keeping up such a lovely home. I feel quite welcome. Yes, quite welcome.

He leaves. MASHA *comes to* ANTON*'s bed, laughs and cries.* ANTON *smiles, pats her head.*

He closes his eyes. She kisses his hand. Lights down. Very slowly.

End of Play

Evgenia, Masha, Olga, Anton. 1902.

Mark Perry teaches playwriting and play analysis at the University of North Carolina at Chapel Hill and serves as a dramaturg for PlayMakers Repertory Company. In 2002, he began Drama Circle, which is dedicated to using the arts to build community.

www.ingramcontent.com/pod-product-compliance
Lightning Source LLC
LaVergne TN
LVHW010106110826
845155LV00028B/509